My Coursework Planner

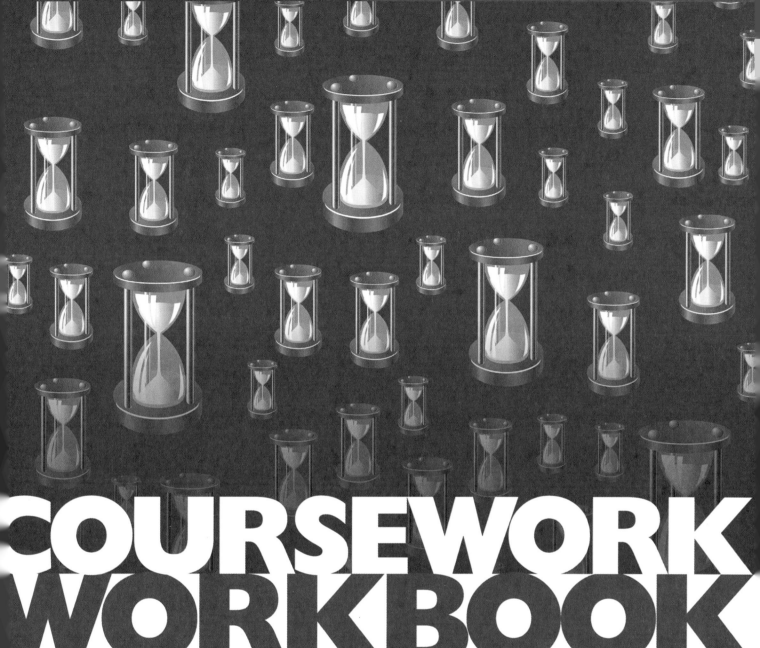

AQA

A-LEVEL

COURSEWORK WORKBOOK

History

Component 3: Historical investigation (non-exam assessment)

Keith Milne

Series editor: David Ferriby

HODDER
EDUCATION
LEARN MORE

The Publishers would like to thank the following for permission to reproduce copyright material.

Acknowledgements

p.34 © 1963 Dr. Martin Luther King, Jr. © renewed 1991 Coretta Scott King, **p.37**t The Wall Street Journal by Dow Jones & Co; News Corporation Reproduced with permission of DOW JONES COMPANY in the format Book via Copyright Clearance Center. **p.39**l, r and b Reproduced with permission of Curtis Brown, London on behalf of The Estate of Winston S. Churchill. © The Estate of Winston S. Churchill, **p.67** Extract from America, Civil War and Westward Expansion by Alan Farmer (Hodder, Access to History, 2015 pages, 108–9). Reproduced by permission of Hodder Education.

Every effort has been made to trace all copyright holders, but if any have been inadvertently overlooked, the Publishers will be pleased to make the necessary arrangements at the first opportunity.

Although every effort has been made to ensure that website addresses are correct at time of going to press, Hodder Education cannot be held responsible for the content of any website mentioned in this book. It is sometimes possible to find a relocated web page by typing in the address of the home page for a website in the URL window of your browser.

Hachette UK's policy is to use papers that are natural, renewable and recyclable products and made from wood grown in sustainable forests. The logging and manufacturing processes are expected to conform to the environmental regulations of the country of origin.

Orders: please contact Bookpoint Ltd, 130 Park Drive, Milton Park, Abingdon, Oxon OX14 4SE. Telephone: (44) 01235 827720. Fax: (44) 01235 400401. Email education@bookpoint.co.uk Lines are open from 9 a.m. to 5 p.m., Monday to Saturday, with a 24-hour message answering service. You can also order through our website: www.hoddereducation. co.uk.

ISBN: 9781510423527

© Keith Milne 2018

First published in 2018 by
Hodder Education,
An Hachette UK Company
Carmelite House
50 Victoria Embankment
London EC4Y 0DZ

www.hoddereducation.co.uk

Impression number   10 9 8 7 6 5 4

Year   2022 2021 2020 2019

All rights reserved. Apart from any use permitted under UK copyright law, no part of this publication may be reproduced or transmitted in any form or by any means, electronic or mechanical, including photocopying and recording, or held within any information storage and retrieval system, without permission
in writing from the publisher or under licence from the Copyright Licensing Agency Limited. Further details of such licences (for reprographic reproduction)
may be obtained from the Copyright Licensing Agency Limited, www.cla.co.uk

Cover photo © valeo5-stock.adobe.com

Typeset in Bliss Light 11/14 by Integra Software Services Pvt. Ltd., Pondicherry, India

Printed in Dubai

A catalogue record for this title is available from the British Library.

Section 1 Introduction

1.1 How to use this book

This book has been designed to help you to develop the skills necessary for success in your Non-examined Assessment (NEA) for AQA A-level History. The book is divided into five sections to illustrate each stage of the process. Each section is made up of a series of topics organised into double-page spreads. On the left-hand page, you will find guidance on what is required to achieve the top grades, while on the right-hand page you will find activities that will help to inform your thinking and practise the skills required for a strong answer. (You may be familiar with this approach if you use the A Level History My Revision Notes revision guides for your examined units). Together the guidance and activities in the book will take you through the skills essential for success.

It is important to have a clear strategy for your NEA. This workbook will help you to achieve this in a planned and logical way. Use this book as the cornerstone of your research and writing – it is designed to be written in so don't be afraid to make use of all the space to refine your ideas and thinking. It will also come in handy when reflecting on your progress in discussion with your teacher.

Please spend some time working through Section 2. Feedback suggests that one of the most important elements of doing well in the NEA is deciding upon a topic, and especially a question, which works well. This is a section not to be rushed. If you have been given a question by your teacher then it is just as important that you fully understand why this is such a good question. Take time to reflect on this section and exactly what your question is asking of you.

Section 3 takes you through the process of locating, deciding upon, and evaluating primary material. You will need to focus on the value of each source in helping you arrive at your answer. This section takes you through the steps to ensure that you focus on the key term '**value**'.

Section 4 is made up of a number of activities that will help you to analyse and **evaluate** the **interpretations** that you use in your coursework. The extracts in this section have been taken from some of the more popular coursework topics, but don't skip over these to look for topics you are familiar with, as each activity has been designed to practise a different skill. The skills involved in identifying arguments, establishing **criteria** by which to judge interpretations and find their flaws are universal and will stand you in good stead regardless of the topic you have chosen for your coursework.

Section 5 looks in detail at how to write up your work and takes you through a structured path from initial plan to finished piece. It considers exactly what the introduction should achieve, how to structure your paragraphs, and also how to integrate the evaluation of sources within your overall **judgement**.

You can find answers to some of the activities online at www.hoddereducation.co.uk/HistoryCoursework/Answers. These have the 'A' symbol to indicate this.

1.2 Key questions answered

What is the coursework about?

The Non-examined Assessment (NEA) is worth 20 per cent of your overall A-level mark and gives you the opportunity to use all of the skills that you have already learned on the two examined units in one piece of continuous writing. This is where you can bring together your ability to consider how convincing an interpretation is and also how valuable a primary source might be and use your **conclusions** to support your answer to a question that covers about 100 years of history. As with any good essay, you will need to have a logical structure where you deploy a balanced **argument** in order to arrive at a very clear judgement. Try to avoid seeing the NEA as just a research task, but instead think of it as a longer style essay in which you use knowledge, interpretations and sources in order to support your own clearly expressed answer.

What can you write about?

Your question can cover any period of history from the Ancient World to the Modern Day as long as it has a date range of approximately 100 years. You may consider themes that you have been interested in, but have not had an opportunity to fully explore yet. For example, you might like to consider the role of women in history or the extent to which individuals have had an impact. Alternatively, you might have a particular topic such as the Tudors or the Crusades that you would like to explore further. There are some restrictions to be aware of however. You need to ensure that your three units, when combined, cover a date range of at least 200 years. You also cannot look at material that you have already studied as part of your examined units, although you can consider the same dates. Section 2 of this book (pages 12–21) covers the detailed considerations around choosing and topic and a title.

How much help can I get?

This should be your independent work and therefore your teacher cannot give you specific advice on how to improve your NEA. However, it is entirely reasonable for your teacher to suggest where you might find the sources and interpretations that you might need. You can also use this book to help you to understand exactly what skills you are expected to deploy and also to give a clear idea of how sources and the interpretations should be evaluated.

How long is the NEA?

Your NEA should be in the region of 3500 words, although there is no set minimum or maximum. However, you should consider that a response substantially shorter than this guidance would struggle to include all of the detailed **analysis** in sufficient depth. If you wrote considerably more than 3500 words then you may become overly **narrative** and descriptive and thereby move away from the type of analysis and focus on the set question, which are the expectations of the higher levels. It is perfectly possible to write an outstanding piece within the guidance of about 3500 words.

What sort of answer is required?

There are a number of key requirements for the NEA.

- Remember it is an 'essay' and requires continuous prose. It must flow as a piece of writing, and you should not use bullet points or subheadings. Paragraphs should be linked together and there should be an obvious line of argument.
- There are no specific marks awarded for the use of English. However, the ability to express yourself clearly and logically is an inherent part of gaining the higher marks. There is no objection to using a spell checker and you have plenty of time to check for typos and misspellings. A clear and readable font like Arial 12 is helpful. **Footnotes** are an indication of a good academic approach, and a **bibliography**, while not specifically marked, is required. There is no expectation of any particular system of footnoting or bibliography as long as the same style is used throughout your NEA.
- It is very helpful if you can identify in your appendix the three primary sources and also the two interpretations that you have analysed and evaluated in depth (though your answer might also refer to others to help substantiate the arguments).
- The key task is to arrive at a clear judgement (i.e. your own opinion), which you ideally identify at the opening of your NEA. You should consider how every paragraph helps to prove the answer that you are advancing. It is worth remembering that marks are not awarded for the actual view that you give, but rather for the manner in which you advance your views. Are your views substantiated (i.e. do you have evidence)?

- The evidence for your views will come from the careful selection of knowledge that is used to challenge or to **corroborate** views. It will also include the analysis and evaluation of both primary and secondary sources to support the view that you are trying to prove.
- Your essay must not only cover the start and end dates of your NEA, but also ensure that there is a good coverage of the dates in between. Your essay should therefore have clear evidence that you are considering the full breadth of the set question. There is no need for the sources to also cover the full date range. However, it can certainly help to achieve overall coverage of the period if the sources are not all on the same few years.

What type of primary source is required?

You coursework essay must contain an evaluation of at least three primary sources. A primary source comes from the period that you are writing about, but does not need to be exactly from the period that you are studying. For example, you might identify the Magna Carta of 1215 as a primary source even if you are considering the period from 1230 onwards as it was still very important in that later period.

At least two different types of primary source should be evaluated. These may be different types of written primary sources, for example official publications, reports, diaries, speeches, letters, chronicles or observations of elite or 'ordinary' people (from the inside or from the outside). Other appropriate sources may include artifacts, archaeological or visual sources, for example newsreels.

When choosing your primary sources consider how easy it will be to evaluate the value of the content, tone and also the provenance.

What type of interpretation is required?

You should write about at least two interpretations. This means finding out about two different opinions or views about the period/question you have set yourself. These views should be from academic historians and not from an A level textbook.

You should be careful to ensure that the interpretations are differing and that they express a clear view. You will also be required to consider the provenance of each interpretation so it is useful to ensure that you can find out about each historian and say something about the time and **circumstances** in which they were writing.

Do I only need two interpretations and three primary sources?

AO2 in the mark scheme only requires that you consider three primary sources, and AO3 requires only two interpretations. You may well decide to use further interpretations or sources to support your overall argument in AO1. Indeed it can be good to use a range of evidence to really prove your answer to the set question. However, there is absolutely no need to evaluate more than two interpretations and three primary sources for AO2 and AO3. To evaluate more will not guarantee higher marks. For more on the mark schemes and Assessment Objectives, turn to page 8.

How is the NEA marked?

This will be marked in school by your teachers. If there is more than one teacher marking the NEA at your school then it will be internally moderated. You will normally be told the provisional marks before they are sent off to the Exam Board. The Exam Board may moderate these marks up or down in order to align your school's results with the national standard. You are told the final confirmed marks on results day.

1.3 The assessment criteria: demystifying the mark scheme

How does the mark scheme work and what are the Assessment Objectives?

The mark scheme for the NEA is designed so that your teachers and also the AQA moderators mark against an agreed set of criteria. The different skills are set out in the 'Assessment Objectives' (AOs). For A-level History as a whole, there are three key objectives that you should be familiar with from your examined units:

- **AO1** concerns knowledge and understanding
- **AO2** concerns your ability to make use of and assess primary sources
- **AO3** concerns your understanding of why the past has been interpreted in different ways – how historians have arrived at different conclusions about the same topic and how to make sense of and weigh those conclusions.

All three of these objectives require you to make judgements and are based on distinguishing different thinking skills. You should already be familiar with these AOs through your work on the examined units.

Your teachers will determine a level and mark for each of the AOs in your NEA.

Below is the wording from the AQA mark scheme. The commentary in the blue boxes will help you to understand exactly what is required.

AO1   20 marks

> AO1 is worth 20 out of a maximum of 40 marks. The allocation of half of the total NEA marks to this AO reminds us that the main purpose of the exercise is to provide an argued and analytical response to a set historical question.

Demonstrate, organise and communicate knowledge and understanding to analyse and **evaluate** the key features related to the periods studied, making substantiated **judgements** and exploring concepts, as relevant, of cause, consequence, change, continuity, similarity and **significance.**

> Analyse and evaluate means that you have considered a view and have compared it to other potential factors.

> A substantiated judgement simply means that you should provide an answer that you have proven with the use of evidence.

> These key concepts should be placed within the chronological context of about 100 years.

Level 5: 17–20 marks

The response demonstrates a very good understanding of change and continuity within the context of approximately 100 years and meets the full demands of the chosen question. It is very well organised and effectively delivered. The supporting information is well-selected, specific and precise. It shows a very good understanding of key features, issues and concepts. The answer is fully analytical with a balanced **argument** and well-substantiated judgement.

> A balanced argument is a key indicator of the top levels. Balance does not mean simply describing an alternate view to the one that you are advancing. Instead, you need to explain why the alternate view is not as valid as the one that you are advancing. You would not therefore completely dismiss an alternate view – simply explain why it is less valid than the view that you are advancing.

Level 4: 13–16 marks

The response demonstrates a good understanding of change and continuity within the context of approximately 100 years and meets the demands of the chosen question. It is well-organised and effectively communicated. There is a range of clear and specific supporting information, showing a good understanding of key features and issues, together with some conceptual awareness. The response is predominantly **analytical** in style with a range of direct comment relating to the question. The response is well-balanced with some **judgement**, which may, however, be only partially substantiated.

You need to be offering a clear answer to the set question. However, even at this high level, you do not need to entirely prove your views.

A good indicator of a response likely to achieve Level 4 or above is that it offers a clear analysis and has advanced some way beyond simply describing the events of a period.

Level 3: 9–12 marks

The response demonstrates an understanding of change and continuity within the context of approximately 100 years and shows an understanding of the chosen question. It provides a range of largely accurate information which shows an awareness of some of the key issues. This information may, however, be unspecific or lack precision of detail in parts. The response is effectively organised and shows adequate communication skills. There is a good deal of comment in relation to the chosen question, although some of this may be generalised. The response demonstrates some analytical qualities and balance of **argument**.

At this level you are beginning to provide an answer to the set question. You have moved away from an overly descriptive response, or one that simply asserts that something is right. You have an argument and you provide relevant information.

Level 2: 5–8 marks

The response demonstrates some understanding of change and continuity but may have limitations in its coverage of a context of approximately 100 **years**. The response may be either descriptive or partial, showing some awareness of the chosen question but a failure to grasp its full **demands**. There is some attempt to convey material in an organised way although communication skills may be limited. The response contains some appropriate information and shows an understanding of some aspects of the investigation, but there may be some inaccuracy and irrelevance. There is some comment in relation to the question but comments may be unsupported and generalised.

A response that fails to cover the full date range set in the question will, no matter how well argued, be limited to this level. It is crucial that you not only consider the start and end dates but that you also cover the full chronological range in-between.

A failure to consider the full demands is most often seen in an almost entirely descriptive response. This is commonly, although by no means exclusively, seen in responses that adopt a chronological structure, beginning with the first date in the set period and simply progressing from one year to the next.

Level 1: 1–4 marks

The response demonstrates limited understanding of change and continuity and makes little reference to a context of approximately 100 years. The chosen question has been imperfectly understood and the response shows limited organisational and communication skills. The information conveyed is extremely limited in scope and parts may be irrelevant. There may be some unsupported, vague or generalised **comment**.

Responses that fail to offer any relevant material will be placed in this level. This includes responses that do not provide any material that can be specifically linked to the dates set in the question.

AO2   10 marks

Analyse and evaluate appropriate source material, primary and/or contemporary to the period, within the historical **context.**

> The demands are the same as for the examined unit. It may therefore help to consider primary sources in the NEA using the same criteria of content, emphasis, tone and provenance as you would for Paper Two.

Level 5: 9–10 marks

Provides a range of relevant and well-supported comments on the value of at least three sources of two or more different types used in the Investigation to provide a balanced and convincing judgement on their **merits** in relation to the topic under **investigation.**

> Comments about the value of a source require you to prove how the source helps to support the answer to your set question. You need to use specific subject knowledge to support your views. For example, it is not enough to simply state that a source is from the time.

> Such comments about the merits of the sources should be in the form of a judgement about whether each source is valuable or not. Value is determined by how well the source helps you to prove your answer to the set NEA question.

Level 4: 7–8 marks

Provides relevant and well-supported comments on the **value** of three or more sources of two or more different types used in the Investigation, to produce a **balanced assessment** on their merits in relation to the topic under investigation. Judgements may, however, be partial or limited in substantiation.

> You need to provide balance to get to this level. This means not seeing a source as being completely valuable, but perhaps identifying that there are reasons not to have complete confidence in its value.

> You should be clear that the value of a source is not the same as its reliability or its accuracy. Indeed, it is possible for a source to be inaccurate but very valuable indeed – for example, a piece of propaganda.

Level 3: 5–6 marks

Provides some relevant comment on the value of three sources of at least two different types used in the Investigation. Some of the commentary is, however, of limited scope, not fully convincing or has only limited direction to the topic under **investigation.**

> You must address the value of at least three sources in order to advance to this level. There must also be two different types of source used.

Level 2: 3–4 marks

Either provides some comment on the value of more than one source used in the investigation but may not address three sources in equal measure or refers to sources of the same 'type'. Or provides some comment on the value of three sources of at least two types used in the investigation but the comment is excessively generalised and not well directed to the topic of the investigation.

> A focus on type might mean making some general comments about how newspapers, for example, are valuable to the historian. In order to advance to the higher levels you need to focus on the specific source that you have chosen.

Level 1: 1–2 marks

Provides some comment on the value of at least one source used in the Investigation but the response is very limited and may be partially inaccurate. Comments are likely to be unsupported, vague or **generalised.**

> In order to access this level you need to refer to the value of at least one source. Ensure that you know what determines the value of a source.

AO3   10 marks

You are expected to discuss how convincing each interpretation is, in exactly the same manner as you have done in the exam. However, there is an added requirement in the NEA that you also consider the time and context in which the historians were writing, plus any limitations that they may have faced.

Analyse and evaluate, in relation to the historical context, different ways in which aspects of the past have been **interpreted.**

This is your opportunity to assess the opinion of other historians. You are not expected to summarise their entire work, simply to find a view (or interpretation) and to use your knowledge to assess how convincing this view may be.

Level 5: 9–10 marks

Shows a very good **understanding** of the differing historical interpretations raised by the question. There is a strong, well-substantiated and convincing evaluation of two interpretations with reference to the time and/or context and the limitations placed on the historians.

To show understanding you must do much more than simply summarise a source – you must be clear about the main thrust of the interpretation and use specific knowledge to challenge or to corroborate it.

Level 4: 7–8 marks

Shows a good understanding of the differing historical interpretations raised by the question. There is some good evaluation of the two interpretations with reference to the time and/or context and the limitations placed on historians, although not all comments are substantiated or convincing.

At this level you will be looking at each interpretation in some depth. There will be a clear criticism of each source and a clear opinion. This opinion will be integrated into the demands of proving an answer to the NEA question.

Level 3: 5–6 marks

Shows an understanding of differing historical interpretations raised by the question. There is some supported comment on two interpretations with reference to the time and/or context **and** the limitations placed on historians, but the comments are limited in depth and/or substantiation.

You need to refer to both the time/context **and** the limitations faced in order to access this level

At this level you will be really trying to address the issue of how convincing each interpretation is in providing a view that helps to advance your answer to the set NEA question.

Level 2: 3–4 marks

Shows some understanding of the differing historical interpretations raised by the question. They may refer to either the time and/or **context** or to the **limitations** placed on the historians, or to both in an unconvincing way.

Limitations might be difficulty in accessing source material due to archives being restricted.

The typical type of response for this level will tend to summarise the interpretation and not really attempt to evaluate how convincing the interpretation is. This is likely to be a very descriptive response.

Time and/or context means that you need to research the historian and find out how the circumstances in which they were writing might have affected their views.

Level 1: 1–2 marks

Shows limited understanding of the differing historical interpretations raised by the question. Comment on historical interpretations is generalised and vague.

Section 2 Making a start

2.1 Choosing a topic

You may be given your topic by your teacher or you may be given the chance to devise your own. In either case, you should think carefully about what makes a good topic and about the reasons for its selection.

1 **If you have a choice, it should reflect your own interests.**

- It might be a topic that covers a period that you have enjoyed studying previously and that you wish to find out a little more about.
- It might be a topic that considers themes that interest you, for example the History of Ideas, Social History or the significance of Military History.
- It might be something that has relevance to your own history and background. It might include events that have shaped your own family history. However, do ensure that there is enough **debate** about your topic from academic historians that you can comment on.
- It might provide you with the chance to study something that is entirely new to you and which you know you are unlikely to have the chance to consider in the set curriculum.
- It might give you the opportunity to consider the history of a continent, country or culture that you have yet to acquaint yourself with.
- It might build upon knowledge that you have already acquired, perhaps looking at a different aspect of a period that you have studied – for example, the foreign policy of a country that you have only studied the domestic affairs of.
- It might be linked to a subject that you are intending to study at university – for example, Economic History, Art History, Literature, Politics or Philosophy.

2 **It should be able to deliver the requirements of the mark scheme and of the specification.**

- You need to ensure that the date range of Component One, Component Two and also the NEA, when combined, covers at least 200 years. This means that the earliest date that you are studying needs to be distanced by 200 years from the latest date that you study. However, you do not need to study 200 **continuous** years.

So, if you study
- Component One: The Tudors 1485–1603
- Component Two: Democracy and Nazism: Germany, 1918–1945

then you have a date range of 1485 to 1945 which is 460 years, so you have already hit the 200-year requirement.

However, if you study
- Component One: The British Empire 1857–1967
- Component Two: Revolution and Dictatorship: Russia, 1917–1953

then you have a date range of 1857 to 1953 which is 96 years. This means that your NEA topic has to go back at least as far as 1767 in order to cover the 200 year requirement.

- You need to ensure that your topic does not include content that you are studying in your examined units, although it can cover the same date range.
- The topic should allow for the development of a question to which there is a clear answer possible within the word guidance.
- You should be able to find a range of sources and **interpretations** to **evaluate** – i.e. there should be conflicting and contrasting evidence for you to weigh up to help you to prove a judgement.

3 **It should be manageable.**

- It should be a topic that it is possible to devise a meaningful question about. You need to be able to produce an answer to your set question within about 3500 words.
- It should be a topic on which you are able to find an academic debate. Sometimes complex topics sound good, but are just too demanding given other calls on your time. It is generally better to produce a complex answer on a straightforward topic than a simplistic answer on a complex topic.
- On the other hand, if you have an enquiring mind, don't opt for a topic that isn't going to offer enough stretch and challenge. Have confidence in your abilities, but be realistic.
- Ensure that you will be able to find primary sources that will help you to advance your answer and to which you can argue a clear case about value.

Mind map

Below is an example of a mind map that a model student has made to map out their priorities in choosing a possible topic.

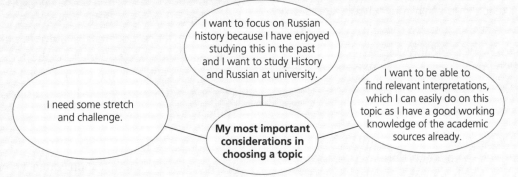

Order of importance:

1   I need stretch and challenge as I know I get bored easily and need to maintain interest in a long project.

2   Though it would be good to study Russian history, if I couldn't find debates I would be happy to look at another aspect of history, such as late-medieval England.

3   Access to interpretations is important. I wouldn't mind venturing a little further than the school library to find them.

My progress

Now use the model above to set out your own priorities. Start by setting out your three highest priorities in the diagram below. The most important considerations for me are:

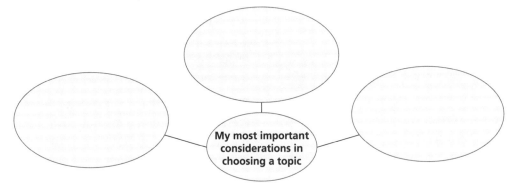

Now list them in order of importance:

1   _____

2   _____

3   _____

2.2 Choosing a title, part 1

Once you have had a topic approved by your AQA advisor, you must decide what specific question you will ask. It is vital to get this right. Remember that you can use your teacher and also your school's Coursework Advisor to perfect the question most likely to fit your needs. Even if you have been told by your teacher which question you will answer, you must be very clear on why this question works.

The question stem

It sounds fairly obvious, but you need to be able to provide an answer to your question. There are some question stems – the beginning of a question – that make it easier to offer a clear answer. Get the stem right and you have already established the basis for a good answer. Good question stems include:

- How far …
- To what extent …
- How important was …
- '[Statement]' How valid is this view?

All of these stems require a clear **judgement** in response. For example, if you are asked 'How important was X …' then you need to actually prove that X was very important, or not at all important, or was important in some regards but not all.

Weaker question stems include:

- Describe …
- What were the reasons for …
- Account for …

While it may still be possible to produce a judgement in response to these weaker question stems, they may encourage a more **narrative** response to your question. Higher marks are awarded for good **analysis**, exactly as for any essay, so you need to avoid questions that encourage you to simply describe events. The NEA is about providing a clear answer to your set question, and providing reasons why you believe in your answer.

Some questions just need a little change in order to ensure a much more analytical response. Therefore 'Account for the decline in royal authority in England in the years 1603 to 1714' might be better expressed as 'To what extent was the decline in royal authority in England in the years 1603–1714 a result of the ambition of MPs in Parliament?'

Choosing appropriate dates

You need to place your question within a context of roughly 100 years. You must write this date range within your actual question. It is important to realise that you will be marked on how effectively you cover the full date range that you have set yourself. Therefore make sure that your dates make historical sense and that there are clear reasons for the start and end dates that you have selected. Let's take the following question:

> 'Martin Luther King was the most significant individual in the development of black civil rights in the USA.' How far do you agree with this view of the years 1865–1981?

This question has a lengthy date range, which doesn't necessarily make arriving at an answer any easier.

The start date of 1865 is the end of the American Civil War and the application of the abolition of slavery across the USA. However, will these events form an important part of the answer to the question? If not, then start the question later.

The end date is the inauguration of Ronald Reagan as President. Will this be referred to in the answer? If not, then it might be better to end with the Civil Rights Act in 1964, or the assassination of King in 1968, which are plainly very important events in the answer to this question.

Getting the stem and the date range right

Consider the following questions. For each question decide if the stem is the best that might be used and if not how it might be improved.

1 What changed and what stayed the same in the development of women's rights in Britain in the years 1815–1921?

_____

_____

_____

2 Discuss the reasons for the rise of anti-Semitism in Europe in the years 1848–1945.

_____

_____

_____

3 In what ways was the emancipation of the serfs in Russia in 1861 important in the improvement in the life of Russian peasants in the context of the years 1855–1964?

_____

_____

_____

4 How does the rise of nationalism in the years 1789–1870 explain the formation of Germany in 1871?

_____

_____

_____

My progress

Now consider the topic area that you are investigating.

What are the start and end dates of your topic?

_____

Why have these dates been chosen?

_____

Can you suggest better start and end dates for your questions and why?

_____

2.3 Choosing a title, part 2

The 'stepping stone' question

Even if you have identified valid start and end dates, you must also ensure that you cover the dates in-between effectively. Some questions make it much more difficult to do this, although they are perfectly valid questions. Responses that consider a few events separated by decades are referred to as stepping stone responses. For example:

> 'The main motivation for those going on Crusade was the pursuit of material gain.' How valid is this view of the years 1095–1204?

The danger here is that the answer will just look at reasons that people went on the first, second, third and fourth crusades, but will miss out the substantial date range in between each crusade. This question would be better expressed as:

> 'The main motivation for those heading to Outremer was the pursuit of material gain.' How valid is this view of the years 1095–1204?

This reformulated question requires an answer that covers the full date range – not just those going on the main crusades.

As the focus of the question is on causation, you could avoid this by looking at longer-term causes of rebellion, for example, social and economic conditions, not just the immediate triggers in particular years.

Is there a double focus?

It is generally better to have a single issue in your question to which you can clearly produce one answer. Sometimes it can be difficult to spot that your question has a double focus until you begin to write your response. For example:

> 'The USA failed to achieve the main aim of its foreign policy which was to stay out of international conflict.' How far do you agree with this view of the years 1898–1991?

With this question you need to define what the main aim of the USA's foreign policy was in the period – a question in its own right. You also need to determine if this aim was achieved – another substantial question.

Is the question too big to answer in about 3500 words?

Some questions are impossible to answer within the recommended word guidance of about 3500 words.

Remember that there are no extra marks for choosing to answer a fancy or clever question. The marks are awarded for answering the question effectively. Therefore, it is in your interests to ensure that the question has an achievable answer.

The following question would **not** be possible to answer in the word guidance:

> In the context of the years 1901–2001, which US president achieved the greatest political, social or economic reform?

Can you find at least two differing interpretations that are relevant to your chosen question?

Before you finally decide on your question, you must do some research to find out if there has been debate among historians about it. AO3 requires you to analyse and evaluate at least two differing interpretations from academic historians. There is no point in beginning to write your NEA if you subsequently find that no historians have written about it. To check this you might do the following:

- Type your actual question into a search engine. Does it produce results that show that your question has prompted debate?
- Use Google Scholar to identify academic works that are relevant to your topic. Use the 'cited by' tool in Google Scholar to check that there is a range of opinion on your topic/question.

Can you find at least three primary sources, of at least two different types, that are relevant to your chosen question?

Before you finally decide that your question will work, you need to be sure that there is a good number of primary sources that you might select. To check this you might do the following:

- Consult the **footnotes** or the appendix of books written about your period. If there is a range of primary sources referenced here then you may well find some that are useful for your own question.
- Search using a website that specialises in primary sources. A good start might be the Internet Modern History Sourcebook. You may well be able to find a good range of primary sources using this website alone.

Strong or weak title?

Look at these questions and write in the box whether you think they are suitable as NEA questions. Consider whether the wording produces a clear task requiring analysis and check whether there is a date range of about 100 years.

Title	Suitable	Not suitable
Assess the reasons for women gaining the vote in the context of the years 1821–1921.		
Individuals were more important than the government in gaining civil rights for black Americans.		
Assess the reasons for Napoleon's downfall in 1814.		
How far was Elizabeth's reign a Golden Age for England?		
Assess the social, economic and political effects of industrial growth on Europe between 1750 and 1900.		
'Gandhi was the most significant factor in the achievement of Indian independence.' How valid is this view of the years 1857–1947?		
How far were accusations of witchcraft in the seventeenth century founded on fact?		

My progress

Has doing the exercise in the activity above affected the way that you think about your own title? Help shape your thinking by filling out the table below.

Topic	Title
What I first thought about my topic:	What I first thought about a title:
What I **now** think about my topic:	What I **now** think about a title:

2.4 Choosing a title, part 3

Here is an opportunity to check the answers to the lists of titles in the activity on page 17. Let's have a look at these titles a little more closely.

1   Assess the reasons for women gaining the vote in the context of the years 1821–1921.

This is not a good title because it could lead to a descriptive list of reasons. Historians much prefer argument and this often means arguing which factor is the most important. In addition, there is no mention of a particular country. A better question might be: In the context of the years 1821–1921, to what extent was the granting of the vote to women in Britain due to the actions of political pressure groups?

2   Individuals were more important than the government in gaining civil rights for black Americans.

The premise of the question is okay, as long as a good chronological context can be addressed in the answer. The question needs dates added to it.

3   Assess the reasons for Napoleon's downfall in 1814.

This question will not work as it lacks a start and end date in the question. In addition, 'assess' as a stem tends to produce narrative responses – it would be better to name a key reason and ask to what extent this was the main factor. This question will not be easy to place in a c100 year context, but it needs this context to be valid.

4   How far was Elizabeth's reign a Golden Age for England?

This is a challenging question. The obvious point is how will this be proven? To establish if this was a golden age we need to compare it to other periods – but what other periods might we choose? This choice of period potentially seems a very arbitrary one, yet we do need to mention a date range in the question. If we set the date range 1485 to 1603 then we may find that there is not enough to debate.

5   Assess the social, economic and political effects of industrial growth on Europe between 1750 and 1900.

This question is too big in scope and would therefore not be a suitable question. It is a huge topic and there are three different questions rolled into one. It would be better to just focus on either the social, economic or political effects rather than all three and to avoid the stem 'assess'. The date range is also too long.

6   'Gandhi was the most significant factor in the achievement of Indian independence.' How valid is this view of the years 1857–1947?

This is a suitable question as it allows for debate and for a clear judgement to be arrived at using a sensible and logical date range.

7   How far were accusations of witchcraft in the seventeenth century founded on fact?

This question has a couple of problems. Firstly, it is far better to name specific dates rather than to just refer to a century. More significantly, the question doesn't make sense. It is really asking if witches actually existed.

My progress

Now is a chance to hone your thinking on choosing a title.

List four possible titles.

1 _____

2 _____

3 _____

4 _____

For each of the titles that you have written above, you will need to ask yourself some key questions. This will help you decide which one to ultimately go with. Take your first possible title and work your way through the questions below. Once you have answered the questions do the same for the other possible titles.

Is the stem of the question suitable? Explain why.

_____

Is there a discussion possible? Explain what it is.

_____

Are there likely to be primary sources available? Indicate why you think this.

_____

Are there different historical views from named historians? Indicate why you think this.

_____

Is this a question with one clear focus? Explain why.

_____

Do the start and end dates make historical sense? Explain why.

_____

Is the question likely to produce a 'stepping stone' response? Explain why not.

_____

Does it make assumptions (e.g. Explain why Napoleon was such a bad ruler) rather than opening up discussion?

_____

Is it possible to provide a clear answer to the question?

_____

Having applied these questions to all of your potential titles you should now have one you feel most confident in pursuing. Write a short explanation about the title that you are now going to go ahead with explaining why it should 'work' and be suitable.

_____

_____

_____

_____

2.5 Unpacking your question

Now you have decided upon your question, you need to make sure that you can establish a clear structure in response and that you can begin the process of acquiring the sources and the interpretations that you will need. However, before you do this you need to read up on the period. The best basis for this is to acquire a general introduction to the period as a whole. Try to start with the general and then narrow down to the more specific.

The aim of this stage of your NEA is to acquire enough information to have a clear idea of what you will be arguing. You are not yet at the stage of acquiring the interpretations and the primary material.

Clearly, you need to decide what the answer to your question is before you begin to acquire the sources and interpretations that will support your answer.

For example, consider the question:

> In the context of the years 1685–1789, how far was the weakness of the individual monarchs the main cause of the French Revolution?

You may have read the introduction to a general book on the period, or you may have done a search online. Perhaps you have found the following:

> The long-term problems for the French monarchy had been obvious for some time – France was spending much more money than it had coming in. This, combined with a taxation system that failed to tax the rich effectively, meant that by 1789 France was bankrupt and needed radical change. However, we should not forget that France had been struggling with money for some time and, as Huskins

> argues, this is not enough to explain why in 1789 there was a revolution. Huskins suggests that it was Louis XVI's inability to support his reforming ministers that was the real problem, and that Marie Antoinette was the driving force behind the instability of the monarchy. On the other hand, Williams argues that it was the ministers that were in fact the problem – it was their ambition that destroyed any hope for reform that might help France. However, Williams does not consider the most obvious culprits in this regard – the Parlementaires. What is clear is that the idea that the revolution was a social revolution, driven by the hungry and discontented poor, is far too simplistic to provide the sole reason for the events of 1789.

This is a good indication that the question will work as there is plainly debate as demanded by AO1, and historians have expressed differing views that can be evaluated, as demanded for AO3. The extract also provides some potential pointers about the paragraphs that might be used.

The extract indicates a good range of potential factors:

- The role of finance, both long term and short term
- The role of Louis XVI and his failure to support reform
- The personal ambition of the ministers
- The ambitions of the Parlementaires
- The revolution as a social revolution.

The question will plainly work. You may now wish to consider what knowledge you need to acquire in order to analyse the role of each factor. It is also time to go on to acquiring the interpretations and sources that will be used, as soon as the decision is made about what you believe the main factor to be.

Unpacking the question

Let's look at your question that you have chosen. Write it below.

_____

_____

How have you started unpacking this? Have you used knowledge gained from previous study? Have you done an internet search? Have you looked at the introduction to any specialist books on the topic? Have you looked at a textbook or something like an *Access to History* book and just glanced at the introduction or chapter headings to get an idea of a possible range of arguments? Write your thoughts below.

_____

_____

_____

Summarise briefly what the range of arguments are:

_____

_____

_____

Now state briefly what you think the answer to your question is. A one sentence answer is best.

_____

_____

_____

Indicate how you intend to cover the full date range set in the question – for example, which of your factors are relevant for the whole period?

_____

_____

_____

Now indicate what evidence you think you will need in order to prove your answer. For example, will you need statistics to back up your answer?

_____

_____

_____

_____

_____

Section 3 Interpretations

3.1 Interpretations: an introduction

What is an interpretation?

An **interpretation** is just an opinion given by an historian. It is not a description of events, it is a point of view. You will have already learned that the study of History is not about factual recall alone, but it is about being able to express an opinion that is supported with factual evidence. In this respect your essays, if written well, are also an interpretation – your own view or interpretation that is supported with evidence. In the mark scheme AO3 asks you to identify and **evaluate** the interpretations advanced by historians.

For the purposes of the NEA, you need to analyse and evaluate two contrasting interpretations. These should come from published academic work – for example a book, or an article from an academic journal. A-level textbooks do not count.

What should you do with the interpretations?

AO3 measures how well you evaluate the interpretations of historians in your NEA. The requirement is similar to that in Component One and so you should be very familiar with the demands. As in Component One, you need to **assess** how convincing the interpretation is. However, the NEA adds a few more elements to these demands, which you must address. These extra elements for the NEA are described below.

Show an understanding of the limitations placed on historians

The typical limitation that you might discuss here is the difficulty that historians had in acquiring the primary sources and the evidence to support their view. For example, historians writing in the 1970s about the 1917 revolution in Russia might not have been able to access a good range of sources because they were unable to visit the archives in the Soviet Union.

Show an understanding of the significance of the time and/or context in which a historian writes

This is quite a demanding element. You need to research the historian but also the date in which the interpretation has been published – even if this date is considerably after the period that you are studying. For example, to evaluate an interpretation written in the 1980s but about the 1200s would require that you do some research about the 1980s and consider what type of audience the historian might be writing for and how this might have affected the interpretation itself.

Compare and evaluate differing historical interpretations

You must ensure that the interpretations are differing, although they do not need to be completely different. Your task then is to compare the two interpretations, bringing in commentary about the content and the provenance. Perhaps the best way to think of doing this is to find an interpretation that supports your answer to the overall question and compare this with a view that is slightly less convincing that you can argue against. Because you need to compare, it is likely that your two interpretations will be considered next to each other in your NEA.

Your task can therefore be broken down into the following:

- Identify what the interpretation is saying. What is the thrust of the interpretation that you have chosen?
- Assess how convincing this interpretation is by using specific knowledge in exactly the same manner as you would on Paper One.
- Integrate the **provenance** of the extract, thinking about time/context and limitations and how these have affected how convincing the individual interpretation is.
- Ensure that you have compared the two interpretations and that you have a clear **judgement** about how convincing they are.

Identifying interpretations

Read the following three extracts on anti-Semitism in Europe.

Extract A

For Structuralist historians, there had been a long standing anti-Semitism in Europe. This was plainly expressed in the pogroms in Russia in the 1880s, but was firmly seen also in the late nineteenth century in France. For these historians, it was society itself rather than individuals within it that accounts for the widespread anti-Semitism. This means that Structuralists consider that there was a slowly evolving distrust of Jews rather than something that suddenly hit Europe in the 1930s.

Extract B: Daniel Goldhagen, *Hitler's Willing Executioners* (1996)

The men and women who peopled the institutions of genocidal killing were overwhelmingly and most importantly Germans. This was above all a German enterprise; the decisions, plans, organizational resources, and the majority of its executors were German. Comprehension and explanation of the perpetration of the Holocaust therefore requires an explanation of the Germans' drive to kill the Jews, because what can be said about the German cannot be said about any other nationality or about all of the other nationalities.

Extract C: Ulrich Wyrwa, *The Making of Antisemitism as a Political Movement. Political History as Cultural History (1879–1914)*, edited by Werner Bergmann (2012)

The reason for the emergence of antisemitism must be seen in the larger transformations taking place in 19th century Europe, in the social conflicts, economic upheavals, cultural dislocations and social-moral crises. Antisemitism, therefore, originated from the 'great transformation', the upheaval of the whole way of living in the formation of the industrial world. This transformation led to a 'clash of economic mentalities', and parts of the middle classes and of the peasant population adhered to the 'moral economy' of the traditional world. Unable to grasp the new capitalist mentality, they accused the Jews of being responsible for this transformation.

Which extract mainly offers an interpretation?

_____

_____

_____

Which extract mainly describes the events?

_____

_____

_____

Which extract mainly explains the view of a 'school of history'?

_____

_____

_____

Which extract would you consider to be the most suitable to use in your NEA and why?

_____

_____

3.2 Identifying and summarising interpretations

This may seem to be a straightforward task but the key point here is that you are looking for opinions and views, not simply facts. You should not for example suggest that an interpretation 'argues that William fought at the Battle of Hastings in 1066'. This is not an **argument** and it is not an opinion, but it is a fact. If the extract had argued 'William was lucky in his eventual victory at Hastings in 1066' then this is indeed an opinion, or interpretation of the past, and it is this that you need to evaluate using your knowledge.

You should be reading interpretations not simply to find out what happened, but to discover what the historian's view or interpretation is of the issue you are studying. Most books will contain the same information. What will be different is their view, interpretation or even just emphasis on different factors or issues. It is those that you need to identify, as they will be what you will evaluate to meet the demands of AO3.

Having identified the view, you should now summarise it in your own words. This is a challenging skill in its own right and requires you to show that you understand what points the historian is attempting to make. Before you can suggest whether the interpretation is convincing or not, you need to prove that you understand what it is.

Looking at the larger picture

There is one important word of caution. When you are identifying arguments in different secondary sources and want to use them in your investigation then remember that simply 'cherry-picking' a word, such as 'powerful' or 'important', or even a short phrase, such as 'Bismarck was a master-planner' does not really count as an interpretation. After all, the writer might have said 'However, Bismarck was not a master planner' and you have simply chosen to focus on the other part of the sentence that offers a completely different view. You would also then find it very difficult to locate evidence from that secondary source to support the argument he was a master planner if actually the writer was arguing exactly the opposite. Make sure therefore that you consider the whole passage or section so that you do have a clear and accurate understanding of the writer's view.

An example of the problems caused by failing to look at the larger picture given by the writer can be seen from the following extract about the Pilgrimage of Grace:

> The common view sees the rebellion [The Pilgrimage of Grace] as the protest of a whole community – 'northern society' – against the breach with Rome and especially the Dissolution of the Monasteries, against new learning and the King's autocracy, complicated by the social and economic grievances of its various component parts …

If you stopped there you would get the impression that the writer is arguing that the rebellion was caused by religious grievances, the claims of the king and made worse by social and economic issues.

The next paragraph continues:

> However, the Pilgrimage originated in a decision by one of the court factions to take the battle out of the court into the nation …

In other words, the real view of the writer is that the cause of the rebellion was court faction, which is then developed.

Now consider the following interpretation about the Pilgrimage of Grace:

Extract A: G.R. Elton, *Reform and Reformation* (1977)

Thus the Pilgrimage originated in a decision by one of the court factions to take the battle out of the court into the nation, to raise the standard of loyal rebellion as the only way left to them if they were to succeed in reversing the defeats suffered at court and in Parliament, and in forcing the King to change his policy.

You should be able to summarise the view of the source about the causes of the Pilgrimage of Grace. For example:

Geoffrey Elton is putting forward the view that the rebellion was due to court faction. The faction had lost its influence at court and had decided that the only way to regain its influence was through a rebellion that would defeat their opponents and force the king (Henry VIII) to change his policy. The source is arguing that the rebellion was due to high politics at court and not due to religion.

Now summarise, in one short sentence, the following interpretation about the role of Empire in the Twentieth Century:

Extract B: N. Ferguson, *Empire* (2003)

The Empire that rules the world today is both more and less than its British father. It has a much bigger economy, many more people, and a much larger arsenal. It is an empire that lacks the drive to export its people and its culture to those backwards regions which need them most urgently and which, if they are neglected, will breed the greatest threats to its security. It is an empire in short that dare not speak its name. It is an empire in denial.

_____

_____

My progress

Select one of your interpretations. Summarise it below in your own words.

_____

_____

_____

_____

_____

_____

_____

_____

_____

_____

3.3 Choosing which interpretations to use

Having identified a range of interpretations, and summarised them in a manner that proves you understand the main thrust of each one, you should decide which you are going to use for AO3 in your NEA.

It is useful to consider that AO3 only requires the in-depth evaluation of two interpretations. There is little benefit to using more than two, and indeed you may not have the space within your NEA to do so. However, you may still wish to use other interpretations to assist you in proving your answer – don't feel that you need to evaluate each interpretation in the depth required for AO3.

AO3 requires that the two interpretations are differing, although they do not need to be entirely different. The easiest way to go about this is to find an interpretation that supports your own view. This interpretation does not need to be an entire book, but can be as short as a paragraph from any academic article that expresses a clear opinion on your topic. It might be helpful if your selected interpretation also argues some things that you do not agree with as strongly – this will help you to balance your views. Summarise this interpretation in as short a sentence as you can. This can then become the basis for finding an alternative interpretation that says something that is differing. If you find it difficult to locate a clear interpretation within the extract then it may be better to find another extract. You are looking for a clear view, which you can either challenge or support using specific subject knowledge.

You may find a number of interpretations, all with slightly different views. The greater the difference in these views the better as it makes your NEA that much easier to argue. You might think that the two obvious interpretations to use will be the ones with the most pronounced differences. However, you also need to consider what might be said about time/context and limitations.

Your next task is to ensure that there is enough material that you can use in relation to provenance. If both of your interpretations are from roughly the same period and the historians have the same background then it may be quite difficult to produce a convincing argument. The best structure might be to have identified a clear difference between the arguments in each extract which you then explain by referring to the time/context and limitations. Things to think about include considering if the date is in some way significant, or if the author has a particular reputation that may affect the message that they are seeking to convey. This is perhaps most obvious in areas that cover controversial topics or ones that have provoked more **debate**.

Limitations might include difficulty in accessing source material but might also include limits placed on the historian by the audience to whom the work has been addressed. A book aimed at the mass market, for example, is much less likely to offer the type of detailed factual support that might be offered by a historian writing for a solely academic readership.

Deciding which interpretations to use

A table may be the best way of easily identifying which interpretations you might wish to use for your NEA. You do not need to have an in-depth understanding of each extract, but this will give you the opportunity to compare and contrast interpretations based on a quick overview before you then devote time to considering a few in much more depth.

Complete the table below.

Title of interpretation/ author	Summary of interpretation	Time/context in which written and possible limitations	How the interpretation links to your overall argument	How this extract differs from the others

Now, looking at your completed table, decide upon the two interpretations that you will evaluate in depth for AO3. Ideally you should choose the two that clearly help you to advance your overall argument, but which also have a clear provenance that you can comment upon. If none of your interpretations seems to have much to say about time/context and limitations then you need to look for other interpretations, or at the worst change your title.

The first interpretation I have chosen is:

_____

_____

The second interpretation I have chosen is:

_____

_____

3.4 Applying knowledge and using argument to support or challenge interpretations

Evaluating the content of the interpretation

The key here is to evaluate each interpretation and to advance much beyond a simple description of content. There are certain phrases and words that you can incorporate into your answer in order to ensure that you remain focused on evaluation rather than simply description (see the box at the bottom of this page).

It is unlikely that you will come across an interpretation that is factually inaccurate. These are after all published interpretations from academic historians. However, you may find that the information used to support an interpretation is weak, misdirected or is just too general to persuade you that the interpretation is convincing. You should use your own specific knowledge to challenge or **corroborate** the interpretation, and the quality and depth of the supporting information provided by the historian. Try to avoid using basic phrases such as 'I know this to be true' or simply asserting that the interpretation is accurate. You

need to think carefully about how the interpretation helps you to advance your overall answer. Remember that you are supporting interpretations that support your own view, and challenging those that are less convincing. Lead with a clear argument and use knowledge to support these views. The marks come from offering an evaluation, not from simply telling the **moderator** what is in the extract.

You may find an interpretation to be convincing simply because it agrees with your own view however it is not enough to simply say this. You need to provide a convincing argument stating why this interpretation is convincing. It might be that the argument can be much better supported than any other, or that a large amount of statistical evidence seems to provide good, objective material. Often, although not always, it will be how effectively the historian has supported their view that will lead you to decide whether an interpretation is convincing or not.

Evaluative words and phrases

Words

However	Illustrates
Conversely	Confirms
Although	Endorses
Opposes	Refutes

Phrases

This is supported by …

This is challenged by …

The view is valid because …

The view is questionable because …

The interpretation can be criticised …

The view can be exemplified with the example of …

On the other hand …

His argument rests on the premise that … however …

Too much significance is given to … whereas …

The historian makes a generalisation that excludes …

The evidence to support the claim is not convincing because …

Read the following extract on the First Crusade.

Extract A: Paragraph taken from the work of an academic historian (2012)

The calling of the First Crusade by Pope Urban II in 1095 may be considered to have been motivated by religious objectives. This is plain to see considering that it was the Pope that called the Crusade at a general church council held at Clermont. Not only were the circumstances of the calling of the crusade religious but the motivation of those who actually set off must have been at least in part shrouded in the cloak of religious devotion. The crusaders were travelling to Jerusalem to pray in the Church of the Holy Sepulchre and did so wearing the Cross of Christ sewn onto their tunics. If the crusaders died whilst on crusade then they were granted forgiveness of sins. However, to claim that this was an entirely religious event, or indeed that the crusaders were mainly motivated by religion, is much more difficult to prove. The younger sons of Europe, aware that they stood to inherit little, had nothing to lose by heading east. The appeal of military glory must also have been a substantial consideration for the young, desperate to break free from the restrictive society of Western Europe. In addition, at least half of those that travelled on crusade did so as servants of the wealthy and so had very little choice over their own travel arrangements.

Having read the interpretation, consider the two student responses below. What is the difference between the two responses? Which simply describes a view and which evaluates a view? Identify where the own knowledge is directly linked to the source.

Response A

The interpretation suggests that the crusaders set out largely for religious reasons and reminds us that the crusade was called by the head of Christian Europe, Pope Urban II. Here the extract indicates that not only the calling of the crusade at Clermont, but also the individual motivation of each crusader was probably religious in nature. The evidence provided for this claim is that the crusaders were heading to the Church of the Holy Sepulchre and did so wearing crosses. However, the interpretation also suggests that there were other motivations such as the desire to claim land or indeed military glory: 'the appeal of military glory must also have been a substantial consideration'. More interestingly, the interpretation also indicates that many of those travelling east did so against their will. Overall this is a convincing interpretation as it gives a clear idea of why people wished to head off on crusade.

Response B

The interpretation suggests that there was a range of reasons for people going on crusade, including religion, the desire for land and the pursuit of military glory. This is a convincing argument simply because if we credit medieval chroniclers with the estimate of about 60,000 people heading from Europe to the East in the years 1096 to 1099 then it would surely be difficult to ascribe one motivation for them all. The author is quite correct to suggest that the actual calling of the crusade had religious overtones, most obviously supported by the fact that this was originally announced at a church council. However, this is not entirely convincing evidence as the speech was given at the tail end of the council, after many representatives had already departed. Moreover, the source fails to consider any political motivation from the Pope especially in the context of the Great Schism. While the actual argument about a range of reasons is convincing, the evidence provided for this is not. There is no support for the view that military glory was a motive – how anyway might this be proven in the years before courtly literature? More tellingly, the suggestion that the disinherited of Europe made up a large number of those heading east has roundly been disproven as the majority of those setting off were those, such as Baldwin, who had to place their extensive lands in trust or sell up before they headed off.

3.5 Evaluating the time/context and limitations of the interpretation

It is absolutely vital that you devote some time to evaluate the time, context and limitations of the two interpretations you have chosen. Indeed, a failure to consider this in any way will limit your response to AO3 to the lowest level – Level 1 (see Demystifying the mark scheme on page 11).

Any interpretation is a product of many factors. Most obviously, the historians are trying to convince you, the reader, that their view is the convincing one, but in our assessment of this we can also consider the background of the historian and determine if there is a particular reason that they may see the past in a certain way. In addition, we might consider the type of audience that they are writing for and how this may have affected the content. At times, historians are also limited by factors outside of their control, for example the ability to access original sources, and this becomes something that further affects how convincing we find an extract to be.

Try to move beyond the type of assessment that you made at GCSE. So generic commentary such as the points below is best avoided:

- The historian is British and therefore is reliable.
- The historian works at the University of Oxford and so is very good.

- The historian is from the country they are writing about and therefore knows a lot about it.
- The book has been published several times and is therefore very reliable.

Instead, try to do some research on the actual historian, perhaps by typing their name into Google to consider precise evidence about their academic background. You can then use this to support any arguments about how convincing you find your extract to be. In addition, if your historian was writing a considerable time ago then there may be an obituary available that summarises some of the points that you may wish to use. In addition, search for book reviews – what have other historians said about the book and the historian?

Remember to integrate your findings about time/context and limitations into a broader argument about how convincing you find the extract to be in helping you arrive at your answer to your NEA question. It is unlikely that you will be suggesting that an interpretation is entirely without merit, otherwise why would you include it in your NEA?

My progress

Produce a 5-minute presentation about a historian who wrote one of the extracts that you found out about earlier.

Firstly, search for as much information on your historian as you can:

- Is there an obituary?
- Has the historian written a series of articles and books?
- What type of reviews have these articles and books received?
- Have you done a simple internet search of your historian?
- Does the historian have a specialism?
- If your historian is still alive, does he or she hold an academic position?
- Has your historian produced a web page (academics often do as part of their institution's website).

Next, consider how you might present this information to the class. You need to explain how this information might help you to arrive at **conclusions** about how convincing your historian is **with reference to your NEA question.**

Consider the following information that a student has researched about a historian.

J. Barnaby, *The New Chinese Dragon, China in the Twentieth Century* (2014)
Barnaby currently lectures at the University of London in the School of Oriental and African Studies. His academic career has stretched over 20 years. The most famous book that he published was an in-depth biography of Chairman Mao, and this received the Fitz prize for History in 1998. Barnaby spent a good deal of his academic career in China and was associate professor of History at the University of Beijing between 2005 and 2011. *The New Chinese Dragon* has been very positively reviewed although the period of the early 1980s has been much less positively received due to gaps in the chronology. Barnaby himself admits in his introduction that there is still much that lies undiscovered, especially in the period immediately after the death of Mao. China, he claims, remains a society careful to ensure that its history is told accurately.

Now consider the two student responses below. Which is a better response to the time/context and limitations requirement? Why? How might the better reponse be improved further?

Response A

Barnaby is an academic working at a prestigious university and therefore he is hardly likely to get things wrong. He will have checked information before his book was published. The fact that this book was published in 2014 makes it more accurate as he will have had time to reflect on the events of the past. It is possible that Barnaby was an eyewitness to some of the events that he describes, therefore making his book even more reliable. He is plainly very enthused and excited by Chinese History which makes this extract even more convincing as Barnaby himself suggests that there is still much to discover in Chinese History. It is unlikely that Barnaby has written this book simply to make money and so this is even more reliable. He takes pride in his work.

Response B

The overall conclusions about the convincing nature of the content of this extract are reinforced by the positive provenance. Barnaby is plainly an expert in his field. To hold a position at SOAS is notable as not only does this suggest that he approaches his work with academic rigour, but also that he does so in an institution with a world-renowned specialism in the area. His academic reputation therefore depends upon producing work that accords with the standards set in the highest of institutions. The fact that he held a position at Beijing also suggests that he is well respected in his field, and possibly that he is able to use language skills to read original sources. It might be suggested that his position at Beijing is evidence that Barnaby was reluctant to upset the Chinese government, but it should be noted that he wrote *The New Chinese Dragon* some time after he left China, and anyway the content of the book is hardly complementary of the Chinese government of the period. This makes his views all the more convincing. However, a note of caution might be that Barnaby himself concedes that some archive material is still inaccessible, and this may well be why the 1980s in his book – no doubt involving the Tiananmen Square Massacre – has received less enthusiastic praise from reviewers. Nevertheless, overall the provenance supports the convincing nature of this extract.

My progress

Select a secondary source relevant to your own question. Write a paragraph that evaluates the source, bringing in relevant and accurate own knowledge.

Section 4 Primary sources

4.1 Finding primary sources

You need to include at least three primary sources in your NEA, two of which should be different types. Each primary source will probably illustrate a particular event or theme to support your overall answer to the NEA. Because the primary sources will most probably cover different events or themes, it is likely that they will not all be referred to together in your NEA, but will instead be spread throughout your response. There is no need to compare the primary sources. You can use a good number of sources to support your **argument** throughout the NEA, but remember you only need three for AO2.

Before you begin to search properly for your sources you need to be very clear about what you hope the sources will do. You should have already decided what the actual answer to your NEA is. You know what points you are trying to prove. You should now set about finding your primary sources with a clear purpose in mind, which is to support your overall answer. The task is not to find the most outlandish or obscure source, nor is it to collect a large number of sources that you simply then describe.

Consider the following points when researching:

- How will this primary source fit into my overall argument? Can I use it to prove my points?
- Is there enough to **debate** about **value** in the content of the source?
- Is there enough to comment on about the provenance/tone of the source?
- Are there three sources of at least two different types that I can use (for example, diaries, newspapers, speeches, cartoons, photographs, chronicles)?

It may be that, if your school has directed you to a certain question, your teachers will already have an idea of where you might need to look to find relevant sources. Also consider asking your library staff about access that your school may have to online resources and subscription-only websites.

To begin with, a simple Google search will be your best approach and will indicate if you are likely to find enough primary sources of different types to be able to advance with your title. For example, if your topic is the British Empire, then type: 'primary sources, the British Empire' into your search box and you will get results similar to those below.

The National Archives | Education | British Empire | Living in the British ...
www.nationalarchives.gov.uk › Education › British Empire ▾
If you have looked at the first case study in this gallery, you will have seen **sources** that give a British view of life in the **British empire**. In this case study you will examine a range of **sources** that look at life in India under British rule. Study each of the **sources** carefully and look for ways in which they support or contradict the ...

British Empire | The National Archives
www.nationalarchives.gov.uk › Education ▾
British Empire resource uses uses **documents** from the National Archives to study the history of the empire in North America, Africa, India and Australia.

Primary Sources - History 065: Great Britain And The British Empire ...
researchguides.library.tufts.edu/c.php?g=452931&p=3093854 ▾
18 Oct 2017 - **British** History Online is the digital library containing some of the core printed **primary** and secondary **sources** for the medieval and modern history of the **British** Isles. Created by the Institute of Historical Research and the History of Parliament Trust, we aim to support academic and personal users around the ...

History in Focus: Empire - Web Resources
https://www.history.ac.uk/ihr/Focus/Empire/web.html ▾
The content is divided into three galleries, which cover the rise of the **British Empire** in the seventeenth and eighteenth centuries, life in the **British Empire**, and its end in the twentieth century. In each gallery there is a set of digitised **primary sources**, including maps, letters, images and documents, published with background ...

Primary Sources - British Empire - LibGuides at Duke University
https://guides.library.duke.edu/c.php?g=289522&p=1930180 ▾
8 Dec 2015 - Full-text database containing **primary** source documents about the **British Empire**. Guardian and The Observer The Guardian (1821-2003) and its sister paper, The Observer (1791-2003) provide online access to facts, firsthand accounts, and opinions of the day about the most significant events of the day.

Primary Documents - HIST 339: History of the British Empire - Earlham ...
library.earlham.edu/BritishEmpire/primarydocs ▾
17 Oct 2017 - Contains 7,247 books, 80 serials, more than fifteen manuscript collections, & court records from the from the late 15th through the to the present. Material published through partnerships with the Amistad Research Center, Oberlin College, Oxford University, & many other institutions. ProQuest Historical ...

British Empire Sources, Documents, Advertising, Media, Film
www.britishempire.co.uk/media/media.htm ▾
Rival European powers (plus the USA) tended to be highly critical of the **British Empire**. ... Some of this criticism no doubt represented rivalry; some of it was aimed more at Britain herself; some was genuinely critical of British policies that led to wars or famines or misuse of local ... Is it a **primary** or secondary source?

Finding primary sources

Consider the websites found in the screenshot on page 32.

Which website would you visit first and why?

_____

Which website do you consider to be the least promising and why?

_____

The National Archives site offers a case study. What are the advantages and the disadvantages of such case studies?

_____

The ranking of sites from a Google search means that the most visited sites, those that have been amended most recently and those that link to most other sites will always appear at the top of a list. Why might this mean that the first sites listed are not always the best for your research?

_____

_____

My progress

Having completed the activity above, now is your chance to map out your own work on finding primary sources, in relation to content.

My provisional title:

_____

_____

Does a simple search indicate that there are enough sources with good content to continue with this title?

_____

_____

Does a simple search indicate that there are enough sources of different types to continue with this title?

_____

_____

Have you checked that these sources are publically accessible and do not require a password or subscription to access?

_____

_____

4.2 Using primary sources to reinforce your answer

It is important to remember that the purpose of using primary sources is to support the answer that you are advancing to your question. The primary sources provide the evidence to support your judgement in the same manner as the interpretations and also your knowledge. You must therefore think hard about what the source is saying and how you will use that information in your overall judgement.

For example, if you are considering the question

> 'Martin Luther King was the most significant factor in the development of black civil rights in the USA.' How valid is this view of the years 1865–1968?

you may have found the following three primary sources.

Source A: Franklin D. Roosevelt, *Executive Order 9346 Establishing a Committee on Fair Employment Practice*, (May 27, 1943)

By virtue of the authority vested in me by the Constitution, and as President of the United States and Commander in Chief of the Army and Navy, I do reaffirm the policy of the United States that there shall be no discrimination in the employment of any person in war industries or in Government by reason of race, creed, color, or national origin, and I do hereby declare that it is the duty of all employers, including the several Federal departments and agencies, and all labor organizations, in furtherance of this policy and of this Order, to eliminate discrimination in regard to hire, tenure, terms or conditions of employment, or union membership because of race, creed, color, or national origin.

Source B: Martin Luther King, Jr., *Letter From a Birmingham Jail* (1963)

In any nonviolent campaign there are four basic steps: collection of the facts to determine whether injustices exist; negotiation; self purification; and direct action. We have gone through all these steps in Birmingham. Racial injustice engulfs this community. Birmingham is probably the most thoroughly segregated city in the United States. Its ugly record of brutality is widely known. Negroes have experienced grossly unjust treatment in the courts. There have been more unsolved bombings of Negro homes and churches in Birmingham than in any other city in the nation. These are the hard, brutal facts of the case. On the basis of these conditions, Negro leaders sought to negotiate with the city fathers. But the latter consistently refused to engage in good faith negotiation.

Source C: *Civil Rights Act* (1866)

All persons born in the United States are hereby declared to be citizens of the United States; and such citizens, of every race and color, without regard to any previous condition of slavery shall have the same right, in every State and Territory in the United States, to make and enforce contracts, to sue, and give evidence, to inherit, purchase, lease, sell, and hold property, and to full and equal benefit of all laws as is enjoyed by white citizens.

Each of these sources seems to indicate that different factors are very important in the progression of black civil rights. Source A suggests that it was the American President, Source B that it was Martin Luther King, and Source C suggests that it was the US Government. The task here is not to describe each source in turn but to integrate the sources into the NEA argument. Hence, if the argument is that King was indeed the most important factor, then Source B can be used to provide further evidence to reinforce this view. The message of the other sources is not dismissed but simply used as part of the argument explaining why the other factors were not as important.

My progress

In your chosen topic find a key argument (e.g. Martin Luther King was the most significant factor, or finance was the main cause of the French Revolution) and then identify the evidence from the primary sources that will support the view.

Key argument in your NEA:

_____

_____

Title and origin of source:

_____

_____

Evidence from your primary source to support that view:

_____

_____

_____

_____

_____

_____

_____

_____

_____

_____

_____

_____

_____

_____

_____

_____

_____

_____

4.3 Evaluation of the value of primary sources using provenance

You will be used to evaluating the provenance of a source from Component Two of your A-level course. Your evaluation in the NEA is very similar indeed and you should use the same advice and skills that you have already learned to enable you to access the higher levels in AO2 of the NEA mark scheme (page 10).

Your key objective is to come to an opinion about the **value** of the source. The value of a source is determined by how well it assists you in arriving at an overall answer to your NEA question.

Things you might consider for each factor

As in Component Two, you will need to consider the full range of provenance when considering the value of the source. This range might include the author, the date it was written, the type of source and the intended audience or the purpose of the source. It is unlikely that you will need to examine every factor, but you should select the factors that help you to arrive at a judgment about value. There is little point in referring to the purpose of the source, for example, if there is nothing that can be said about how this affects value.

The author

Is the author an important individual whose views are a valuable insight into a key aspect of your period? Was he or she a member of an important group or movement providing evidence of the aims and beliefs of a wider range of people?

The date written

Is your source written just before or after an event that is important in arriving at a judgement about your NEA? Avoid producing the generic response that 'this was written close to the events' but instead use specific knowledge to place the source in its historical context and to arrive at a judgement about its value.

The type of source

Does the type of source affect its value? A diary might make the source more valuable as it provides an insight into the personal thought of a significant individual. A political speech may be valuable in providing an indication of what a party hoped to achieve, or at least what they thought would win votes. Remember, however, that you need to keep your judgement based on the specific source that you are considering and not just write a generalised commentary that could apply to any source of a similar type.

The intended audience

Has the source been affected – either positively or negatively – by the intended audience? If the source has been written for a wider audience then you might say that the value is that it reflects the mood of a large number. It may be that the intended audience – especially if an important individual or group – may be the very thing that makes the source valuable as it provides an insight into their views.

The purpose of the source

Some sources, such as speeches and political manifestos, are designed to persuade the reader to do something – this might make them valuable. Other sources, such as letters or reports, might be designed simply to inform and can also be very valuable for this reason.

How to determine value

Value is about how much the source helps you to develop the answer to your NEA question. It is not enough to simply say that a source is accurate or reliable.

- A source may be accurate and therefore valuable because it provides you with good information about the period.
- A source may be inaccurate and therefore valuable because it gives an insight into why the author wished to mislead the reader – for example, a piece of propaganda.
- A source may be written by one person and therefore valuable because it gives an insight into that key individual.
- A source may be written at a key turning point and therefore valuable as it provides evidence of the emotions that the event evoked.
- A source may be written at a key turning point and therefore not very valuable as it fails to provide objective evidence free from the emotion of the event.

Let's take the example of the Vietnam War. After a long struggle against Communist forces, the USA left Vietnam in 1975. One contributory factor towards the USA's defeat was hostile media and press coverage and the US home front, but how important was this? The three sources on the right offer different viewpoints.

In relation to a question considering why American foreign policy failed in the twentieth century:

1   How does the information about the authors affect the value?

_____

_____

_____

_____

2   How does the type of source affect the value?

_____

_____

3   How does the purpose of the source affect the value?

_____

_____

4   Which source is likely to give the most reliable insight and which source is the most valuable?

_____

_____

5   Is the most reliable or accurate of these three sources also the most valuable?

_____

_____

Source A: In 1995 a senior Vietnamese commander Bui Tin gave an interview to the *Wall Street Journal*. Bui Tin was given the task of leading interrogation of American prisoners of war. He later revealed that some American POWs were tortured.

The antiwar movement was essential to our strategy. Support of the war from our people was completely secure while the American home front was vulnerable. Every day our leadership would listen to world news over the radio at 9 a.m. and follow the growth of the American antiwar movement. Visits to Hanoi by antiwar Americans like Jane Fonda, and former Attorney General Ramsey Clark and ministers gave us confidence that we should hold on in the face of battlefield reverses.

Source B: In 1996 the North Vietnamese commanding officer General Giap gave an interview to CNN and was asked what the key to victory was. He is considered to have been a great military strategist, and he became a prominent political leader in the newly united Vietnam.

The Americans fought the Vietnamese, but they did not know much about Vietnam or anything at all about the Vietnamese people. Vietnam is an old nation founded in a long history before the birth of Christ … [the Americans] knew little about our war theories, tactics and patterns of operation …
We have a theory that is different from that of the Americans. The Americans did not understand that ... As our president said, there was nothing more precious than independence and freedom. We would rather sacrifice than be slaves.

Source C: The journalist Robert Elegant reported the war and recorded his views in the British magazine *Encounter* in 1981. A British-American author and journalist born in New York City, he spent many years in Asia as a journalist and is fluent in a range of languages. He became an advisor to the American President on Asian affairs and Vietnam.

For the first time in modern history, the outcome of a war was determined not on the battlefield but on the printed page and, above all, on the television screen. Looking back coolly, I believe it can be said that South Vietnamese and American forces actually won the military struggle. They virtually crushed the Viet Cong in the South, and thereafter they threw back the invasion by regular North Vietnamese divisions. Nonetheless, the war was finally lost because the political pressures built up by the media had made it quite impossible for Washington to maintain even the minimal material and moral support that would have enabled the Saigon regime to continue effective resistance.

4.4 Evaluation of the value of primary sources using content

There is a difference between using the content in order to reinforce your overall answer to the NEA, and in using the content to make judgements about how valuable the source is. The marks for AO2 are mainly related to how convincing the evaluation of the source is. Let us now consider how to **assess** the value using the content.

The value of the content may be considered by looking at some of the following factors:

- The main thrust or point being made by the source.
- The quality and type of evidence used in support of this point.
- The tone of the source.

The main thrust or point being made

You need to prove that you understand the message of the source. There is little point in attempting to assess value before you have done this. Try to summarise the message or thrust of the source in your own words and avoid lengthy sections of quotation. Excessive quotation just proves that you can extract relevant points; it does not prove understanding. Once you have done this, consider how the thrust or main argument adds value to the source. At the simplest level the source may agree with your own answer to the NEA and therefore it is valuable because of this. However, you should remember that simply seeing a primary source as providing information to support your argument is only one way to prove value.

The quality and type of evidence used in support of this point

The evidence in a source can also be a very good indication of value. The source may be valuable because it provides an extensive amount of accurate information and evidence. The quality and precision of this evidence may be the thing that you feel really gives the source its value. On the other hand, the source may be valuable because of the inaccuracies and gaps in the evidence – these gaps may give you an insight into the purpose behind the source. For example, a propaganda source may have weak or even inaccurate evidence, but this is the very thing that gives the source its value. It provides an indication of what a government agency wanted people to believe about an event or period and how they may have wished to distort the truth in order to achieve this.

The tone of the source

It is important to consider the tone of the source, especially if it is a written source. However, also remember that this is not an exercise in literature appreciation. Your comments about tone are likely to support arguments about the historical value of the content or of the provenance. You need therefore to do more than simply state that the tone is emotive, for example, but must instead prove how this links to your argument about value. You may have identified that the tone is emotive, and would need to quote a couple of key words or phrases to prove that this is the case. However, you must then go further to indicate how an emotive tone affects the value of the source. It may be that the emotive tone detracts from the value as you hope that the source can provide you with good objective information about an event. On the other hand, you might argue that an emotive tone is in fact really of high value because it gives an excellent indication of how the key individual who wrote the piece was so immersed in the events.

Here we are going to consider how we might use the content of the source to address value. In your NEA it is unlikely that all three sources will refer to just one event or theme.

Source A: Churchill writes a private letter to senior RAF commanders expressing concerns about the bombing of Germany, March 1945. Quoted in Nigel Knight, *Churchill: The Greatest Briton Unmasked* (2010)

It seems to me that the moment has come when the question of bombing German cities simply for the sake of increasing terror should be reviewed. Otherwise we shall come under control of an utterly ruined land – the destruction of Dresden remains a serious query against the conduct of allied bombing. I see the need for more concentration upon military objectives rather than more acts of terror and wanton destruction.

Source B: Churchill writes a public letter to the head of Bomber Command, Arthur Harris, on 1 June 1942, after the successful 1000-strong bomber raid on Cologne. This letter was also circulated to the British press. Quoted in James Fyfe, *The Great Ingratitude* (1993)

I congratulate you and the whole of Bomber Command upon the remarkable feat of organization, which enabled you to despatch over a thousand bombers to Cologne in a single night. The proof of the growing power of the British Bomber force is also the herald of what Germany will receive city by city from now on.

Source C: Churchill discusses bombing and possible gas attacks on the Germans at a meeting of the heads of the armed forces in Downing Street, 6 July 1944.

It is absurd to consider morality on this topic when everybody used gas in the last war with no complaints from the moralists or the Church. I want a cold-blooded calculation of how it would pay us to use poison gas. We could drench the cities of the Ruhr and many other cities in Germany in such a way that most of the population would be requiring medical attention.

Look at these two paragraphs and decide which you think better evaluates the value of the sources and why?

Paragraph 1

Churchill was determined to wage war against Germany very rigorously and was not afraid to take drastic measures. This included bombing campaigns. After the 1000 bomber raid on Cologne in 1942, he wrote to the head of Bomber Command Arthur Harris on 'the remarkable feat' of sending a thousand bombers and told him that it heralded further attacks. This is very valuable. Though there were critics, Churchill was not afraid to take difficult decisions in the interests of the war effort. Source B illustrates that Churchill was perfectly willing to support the use of bombing despite his private concerns.

Paragraph 2

Churchill's views are plainly not consistent and thus much of the evidence here cannot be seen as typical but this adds to the value as it reinforces the point that Churchill did indeed respond to prevailing conditions – he was not an ideologue stuck in his ways. It is important to take this into account and we perhaps should not look for consistency in objectives or methods across the Six Year War. Although it could be argued that the war was much closer to being won by then and that by March 1945 Churchill was rightly concerned with rebuilding Europe after the peace, it could also be argued that the exceptionally heavy casualties in Dresden, which was not really a military target, led rightly to doubts. This reinforces the sense that British foreign policy was indeed motivated by a moral dimension thus reinforcing my main argument and the value of this source. The limitations of his greatness can also be seen in his overestimation of the effects of bombing, as expressed in his congratulations to Harris, although the tone of this source does suggest that it was designed more as a propaganda piece and so we should question its value in providing an objective insight into Churchill's actual beliefs.

4.5 Using the skills you have developed to produce a clear argument

We have now considered how the content of primary sources might be linked to the set question and how these sources might be evaluated for value. The next skill to develop is linking these together to ensure that the three sources are both evaluated and also linked to the set question in a convincing and united manner. In order to do this we should remember the skills being assessed:

- The ability to read the source carefully and to use it to help advance your overall judgement about the NEA question.
- The ability to evaluate the content of the source and to come to a judgement about value in relation to the set question.
- The ability to evaluate the provenance of the source and to come to a judgement about value in relation to the set question.

While the evaluation of the value of the sources is very similar to that required in Component Two, the NEA is a lengthy essay and not simply a commentary on a given set of sources, so you need to ensure that your evaluation is integrated into a much longer piece of writing. You are effectively integrating the critical treatment of evidence in an essay.

Let's recap those skills. Let's say that you are investigating the reasons for Tudor Rebellion in the context of the years 1485–1603. You have decided to focus one section of your NEA on whether the rebellion of 1536 against Henry VIII was a religious one. A starting point would be to look at the rebels' demands.

Source A: *The Pontefract Articles* (1536)

The supremacy of the Church in matters of care of souls to be reserved to the See of Rome as before. The consecrations of the bishops to be from the Pope, with a reasonable payment for the outward defence of the Faith.

Reason for inclusion: This shows how important religion was because the rebels demanded a return of the supremacy of the Pope in spiritual matters, even accepting some money would be paid to Rome. Cromwell and Rich were seen as subverting the good law of the realm but also supporting heresy (beliefs that went against the teaching of the Church). So religion was linked to other grievances but given prominence. This might be linked to the overall judgement of your NEA that religion was the main motive in rebellion.

Provenance/value: The Pontefract Articles were intended to rally many people to the cause of rebellion and might have emphasised religious causes to get maximum support, especially as the pace of religious change had been rapid. The framers of the demands in 1536 needed to reflect a range of grievances but stressed religion as a linking factor to get committed support. This may affect the value as it is a statement of intention from a small number, not what perhaps was felt by all. The purpose of the source was however to rally support and this may therefore be valuable in showing us what the framers of the Articles at least thought the major grievances were.

Content/value: The changes to the monasteries had been a major concern in many parts of the country and there was widespread resentment that change had been pushed through by a clique at court. However, there were other causes of discontent, such as concern about the King's control of Parliament and taking money from the North, so this extract does not give the whole picture. Its value is limited due to lack of breadth in comparing one factor to another and even then taking a very narrow view of the type of religious grievance.

Producing a clear, integrated argument

Consider the following brief passage which gives a shortened indication of how Source A on page 40 might be used in an NEA response to the following question:

In the context of the years 1489–1601 how far was rebellion caused by religious concerns?

Religion was obviously an important element in the rebellion of 1536 and the Pontefract Articles issued by the rebels have most of their demands linked to religious grievances, as might be expected as religion was a major motivating element and the demands were intended to justify rebellion and gather support. The content of the source makes very clear the desire of the rebels to change the direction of religious policy in England and this confirms the theme of religion being a consistent motive behind rebellion and even just unease across the Tudor period. However, it was often difficult to separate religion and secular grievances, and the value of this source is somewhat limited in that it only illustrates one type of grievance, and even then only one part of the desire for religious change. The rebels plainly wished to rally as many people as possible to their cause, and, while it might well be valuable to consider that this therefore reflects popular grievance, its value is limited by the sense that it only really indicates the factors that the rebel leaders thought might appeal to the masses. There is little here to prove absolutely that this is the core motive. Hence the value is somewhat limited, but overall it is a fair indicator of at least what popular grievance was felt to be by some contemporaries.

Using three different colours highlight areas of the passage above that:

- use content of the source to reinforce the overall argument of the NEA
- use content of the source to consider value
- use provenance of the source to consider value.

Do you think that the balance of these three components is about right? Explain your decision.

_____

_____

My progress

Find a key piece of primary evidence about your own question.

My piece of primary evidence:

_____

How will the content help to advance your overall answer to the NEA?

_____

Explain how its provenance and content might be used to prove value.

_____

_____

Now try writing a sample paragraph of your essay which integrates all of the above.

5.1 Introduction to writing up

The need to write a good essay

The NEA is, in many respects, simply a long essay in which subject knowledge and the critical use of both primary and secondary sources are used to support a clear and consistent judgement. Half of the marks for the NEA are for AO1, which measures how effectively you convey your judgement and also how well supported this judgement is (see pages 8–9). The remainder of the marks is for the evaluation of the interpretations and of the sources.

As the NEA will be around 3500 words, a clear danger is that the answer loses its focus on the question and moves towards providing a description either of the period or of the sources. It can be difficult to remain focused on providing an answer across such a long piece of continuous prose. It is worth remembering that the selection of the most relevant pieces of knowledge is part of the skill being tested for AO1. The NEA is not simply an opportunity to demonstrate how much knowledge you have acquired.

As for any essay you will need to ensure that you know what answer you are trying to prove before you start writing. It may be useful to write a simple one-sentence explanation of what you are trying to prove just to remind you of the answer to your NEA. You then need to consider how you might go about proving this answer. Like any good essay, you will need to produce a balanced argument in which you consider alternative views. You will also need to fully integrate your critical use of different types of sources and also your interpretations into a consistent line of argument. Finally, you need to ensure that this can be done within a reasonable length of response.

As a useful summary:

- You will need to ensure that there are no parts of the answer where you lose focus on the actual question.
- You will need to ensure that you have effectively covered the full breadth of the question.
- You will need to check that there are no parts where there is just description.
- You need to ensure that you have considered different views and have not produced just a one-way argument.

- You need to ensure that all of your arguments are backed up by detailed and accurate knowledge and that your conclusion follows logically from what you have said in the main body of your answer.
- You need to ensure that your primary sources help you to arrive at an overall judgement.
- You need to ensure that you have considered how valuable your primary sources are in relation to the NEA question.
- You need to ensure that you have compared your interpretations and evaluated how convincing their relative arguments are in relation to the set NEA question.

Ensuring that you have an answer to the set question

The first step to an effective answer is to ensure that you know what your answer will actually be. The next step is to identify what factors you might use in order to support this answer.

A brief plan may look something like this:

Question
In the context of the years 1685–1789, how far were ambitious ministers the main cause of the French Revolution?

Answer
Finance was the main cause of the French Revolution.

Factors
Finance is the only factor that stretches across the whole period. It explains why other factors such as the weakness of Louis XVI and the role of Parliament were so important. Without the financial crisis the other factors would not have been present. The revolution was caused by the bankruptcy of France.

How will you bring all this together? The best way to do this is to ensure that you have a clear, basic plan.

The basic plan

What is your question?

_____

_____

What is the answer to your question?

_____

_____

_____

Identify the factors to support this answer.

_____

_____

_____

_____

_____

_____

_____

Prioritise your factors to indicate your most powerful factual evidence and your least powerful.

_____

_____

_____

_____

Are there any links between the pieces of evidence that you have identified? Does one reinforce another?

_____

_____

_____

Identify which factors each of your sources and your interpretations will best address.

_____

_____

_____

_____

_____

5.2 Developing a detailed plan

A more detailed plan will help you to focus your response further. Now that you have identified your evidence you need to think about the specifics of how this might fit together.

The first stage is to ensure that you have considered all the implications of your question. A good way to do this is to underline or highlight the key words and phrases in your title, perhaps with the dates to be covered in one colour and the key words or phrases in another. This will help you to maintain focus. For example:

> In the context of the years 1685–1789, how far were ambitious ministers the main cause of the French Revolution?

In the activity on page 43 you identified the issues that you intend to cover in your answer, but now you need:

- an outline of the issues or factors you will cover
- the arguments for and against each issue (the balance) and the evidence to support each

- the reasons that one factor might be more significant than the next.

Although most of your marks are for AO1, you do need to use and integrate both primary and secondary sources into your argument. It would be also be helpful if your plan identified which sources will be used where.

Once you have decided upon a main factor – effectively the answer to the set question – then consider how you will approach the demand for balance. It is important that you don't just describe the alternative views but instead explain why the other factors are not quite as important as your main factor – this is a balanced argument.

You might find it easier to do this as a table with a series of columns like the one below. It will give you an overall view of your work and be a useful checklist. Below is an example of a completed chart.

Factor	Evidence in support of this factor being important	Evidence against this factor being important	Sources to help support your argument about this factor	Judgement. How important is this factor?
Finance	1685–1789 Inequitable taxation system. The Farmers General. Compte Rendu. Cost of American War. Turgot's reforms. Calling of Assembly of the Notables. Calling of Estates General.	Taxation system always been inequitable. Debt largely paid off by mid-18th century. Controller generals had proposed reforms.	Primary: Govt. report Compte Rendu. Secondary: Doyle.	Finance was the driving force. EG called due to bankruptcy. France unable to afford to function – needed change. Other factors all linked to trying to solve this crisis
Monarchs	Failure of character. Failure to support reforming ministers. Inconsistent in action. L16 vulnerable to Marie Antoinette. L14 creates image of absolutism.	L16 wanted reform – calling of EG and Assembly of Notables. Let down by ministers. Ambitious wife. Not absolute reluctance to engage.	Primary: Letter to Necker from L16.	L16 an important factor due to failure to support reform. Bereavement led to his disassociation from politics. L14 creates unattainable image. L15 poor decisions, e.g. 1756 and his decision to join the Seven Years War leads to long-term crisis.

Factor	Evidence in support of this factor being important	Evidence against this factor being important	Sources to help support your argument about this factor	Judgement. How important is this factor?
Ministers	Necker made it impossible to enact reform – became caretaker. Maupeou and ministerial despotism. Poor advice Brienne.	Maupeou crisis only period of effective rule. Necker kept state afloat through loans. Physiocrats prove there were new ideas. Crisis was when L14 tried to rule alone.	Secondary: Henshall page 47, para 2.	Ministers generally served the crown well. Were self-interested but this never replaced service. Advancement depended on how well served crown.
Parlement	Compliant under L14, ambitious under L15, fractious under L16. Fundamental Laws. Increased frequency of remonstrance.	Parlement easily exiled. Brienne and Maupeou proved they not major threat. Much less significant after decision on EG voting by estate.	Primary: Fundamental Laws.	Parlement second most substantial issue in long term – not as significant short term. Tried to call King's bluff in calling EG and it failed. Enlightenment used as a cover for self-advancement.

My progress

Create your own table as per the example below. You can complete it on this page or alternatively reproduce it on a larger sheet of paper.

Factor	Evidence in support of this factor being important	Evidence against this factor being important	Sources to help support your argument about this factor	Judgement. How important is this factor?

5.3 Writing the introduction

As for any essay, it is crucial that you write an effective introduction. An introduction to the NEA should be more detailed than that for your examined essays but essentially it does exactly the same job – it provides your answer to the set question.

In providing the answer, the introduction should give an indication of the evidence – whether from your knowledge, the sources, or both – and it should give some sense of the themes or factors that you will be examining. The introduction might also give a clear indication that you are approaching the question with a sufficiently wide timeframe.

Let's take the following question on black civil rights in the USA as an example.

> **How far was Martin Luther King the most important factor in the development of black civil rights in the USA in the years 1865–1965?**

Now consider this shortened version of a potential introduction.

There is a range of reasons for the development of black civil rights in the years 1865–1965. At the opening of the period slaves had just won their freedom and were no doubt expecting to enjoy their newfound equality and to embrace the opportunities offered by post-bellum USA. Yet by 1965, the fact that a new Civil Rights Act was needed just proves how little had been achieved. In fact, it is clear that blacks had to struggle for their rights in this period and so black individuals such as Martin Luther King must have had a role to play in this. Yet there were also other factors such as the role of the US presidents and also the role of the public and the media that must be considered. No factor alone is likely to explain why something happened and so all factors together should be considered. I shall firstly consider the role of Martin Luther King as this was indeed the most significant.

The use of the personal pronoun and signalling what the student will firstly consider is not helpful.

There is material in the sample introduction that is good. The introduction does attempt to offer some awareness of breadth by referring to the start and to the end of the period. However, this is not convincingly linked to the set question. Why, for example, should the need for a Civil Rights Act in 1964 prove that black people alone had to struggle for rights, and more importantly why does it mean that black individuals must have had a role to play? In addition, the introduction uses this information just to suggest that things had not greatly improved in the period, not to give any indication as to what the most important factor in the development of black civil rights actually was. It might also have been useful to refer to some of the evidence – and perhaps even the sources – that might prove the answer that is being advanced by the student.

The introduction is therefore too assertive. This **assertion** continues, as there is then a list of potential other factors with no indication of why they might be significant. As a positive aspect, the introduction does clearly state the answer to the question at the end, but fails to offer any reason at all why this might be the case.

So in summary a good NEA introduction may include the following:

- A clear answer to the set question.
- Evidence that the breadth element is being considered right from the outset.
- An indication of some of the evidence that will be used to support this answer.
- An indication of what other factors will be considered, i.e. the balance, plus some indication of why these factors are less significant than your main one.

Writing the introduction

Now that we have considered some key qualities of a good introduction, look at the shortened introduction below and decide whether it is effective or not and why. Make notes around the introduction using the following questions: Is there a clear answer to the set question? Is evidence identified to support the answer? Is there evidence that a range of factors is going to be considered? How would you improve this introduction?

> 'There was more continuity than change in the style of Russian government in the years 1855–1964.' How far do you agree with this view?

On the surface, there was a major change in the style of Russian government across these years. The tsarist regime was oppressive and based on the idea of divine right rule. There was little scope for the expression of alternative views of government. The communist regime was, at least in theory, more responsive to different approaches, perhaps best seen in the different approach to economic reform, moving from War Communism to the NEP. However, the basics of the style of rule remained the same. It was still one individual that seemed to control all aspects of government. Stalin was little removed from the type of rule seen under Alexander III. The secret police may have changed its name across the period, but it did essentially the same job of oppression and control for central government. Moreover there was the same sort of dismissive attitude to the interests of local government across the whole date range. Taken as a whole, therefore, this period sees more continuity than change in the period with the most telling element of continuity being in the use of the secret police.

My progress

Using the advice on page 46 write an effective introduction to your own question and then indicate why you think it will work for you.

My introduction:

This achieves all of the objectives of a good introduction because

_____

_____

_____

5.4 Avoiding narrative and description

Good history at A-level is all about expressing an answer that is supported by specific pieces of evidence. It is easy to think that history requires knowing a great deal, but in fact the higher levels are awarded to students who have a clear opinion and are able to select pieces of information that are best used support their answer.

The plan you have drawn up should help to stop you just simply telling the story, but it is important that you are clear as to what is meant by **narrative** and description before you start writing.

Look at the following two excerpts from answers to the following question:

> The foreign policy of the USA was motivated entirely by the needs of big business.' How valid is this view of the years 1898–1992?

Which of the two excerpts provides part of an effective answer to the question and which simply tells you what happened?

Excerpt A

In the aftermath of the First World War, the USA failed to join the League of Nations. The League had been established in order to advance the cause of international justice, but especially to preserve world peace and to enact disarmament. The USA's foreign policy quickly returned to normalcy which meant isolationism. Progressivism again became a concern, at least until the 1930s. In the 1930s there was a keen effort for the USA to keep out of war. The Neutrality Acts made it illegal for the USA to join war. The events, especially of the Spanish Civil War and the bombing of Guernica, motivated a desire to keep out of war. On 7 December 1941, a Japanese surprise attack at Pearl Harbor killed over 2300 American servicemen. Franklin Roosevelt then declared war and so America was forced out of isolationism.

Excerpt B

The First World War led to concern that the USA had been dragged into a costly conflict that brought little benefit. The years in which the USA had stayed out of war had been largely beneficial to American businesses as they had taken markets in the petrochemical, automobile and also film industries from the European powers. America's return to normalcy in foreign policy was therefore nothing less than a desire to consolidate the economic gains made in the period 1914 to 1917. While there was a general fear of getting involved in war, perhaps made worse by the events of the Spanish Civil War and the example of Guernica, it was the failure of the New Deal to address the problems of the Depression that shifted the opinion of big business towards the late 1930s. In both cases – the desire to stay out of war and also the eventual decision to join the Second World War – it was big business that was the driving factor behind the foreign policy of the USA.

Extract B is much more directed to the question. It avoids listing events, rather it has sentences that present an argument, and then uses subject knowledge to support this. Extract A is really a collection of unrelated information. At times, the reader must wonder why this information has been included in Extract A as there is no explicit link made to the set question.

So how do you avoid simply telling the story? One of the best ways is to ensure that the opening sentence of each paragraph relates back to the question. This will also help to keep you focused on the actual issues in the question and might stop you writing narrative.

Opening sentences

Read the following possible opening sentences for the question 'The success of the Reformation in Europe in the years 1517–1620 was mainly due to the printing press.' How far do you agree with this view?

Highlight in purple the sentences that introduce an argument related to the question.

Highlight in red the sentences that simply describe an event related to the Reformation.

1   In 1517, a Friar who had become disenchanted by the legal profession announced that the Church needed reform.

2   The printing press was not new, but the development of movable type made it much easier to print pages cheaply thus helping ideas spread much more quickly.

3   Many people in Europe were very sincere Christians.

4   The years 1517–1620 saw the Reformation spread to many of the German states.

5   The Reformation was a reform of the existing practices of the Church and saw the destruction of images such as statues of saints.

6   The Reformation involved a good range of individuals such as Martin Luther, Zwingli and also Calvin.

7   The Reformation latched on to a widespread desire for change, especially among those who had been paying a large amount of money for the upkeep of their local church.

My progress

Having completed the activity above, now apply this to your own title.

Title of my NEA:

_____

What issues are you going to discuss? These have been identified in your plan.

Construct at least one opening sentence for each of the key points your Investigation will discuss. Ensure that the sentence introduces an idea relevant to the actual question and does not simply describe facts.

1   _____

_____

2   _____

_____

3   _____

_____

4   _____

_____

5   _____

_____

6   _____

_____

5.5 Discussion not just explanation

We have addressed the need to answer the question within each paragraph and also the fact that each paragraph should focus on a particular theme or point relevant to the question. This is quite a challenging skill to perfect, as you need to ensure that you are linking your argument within each paragraph back to the set question. There is a big difference between explaining a range of factors or issues and weighing up the importance of those ideas and issues in relation to other explanations of an event. You will also have to ensure that this assessment goes on throughout the essay if you want to reach the very high levels in AO1.

You may wish to introduce an argument in the opening sentence of a paragraph. You will then need to develop this argument before reaching a substantiated judgement. In developing your argument you should consider both sides of the argument.

- What evidence is there to support or challenge your argument? You may bring in primary and secondary sources to support or challenge your argument.
- What are the strengths and weaknesses of the sources you have brought in? They will need to be evaluated, but we will look at integrating primary and secondary sources later.
- Why is one argument more compelling than another? That last point will be your judgement.

Read the following example paragraph which is part of an answer to the following question.

1 In the context of the years 1848–1939, how far was the outbreak of the Second World War due to long-term German expansionism?

An important factor in the outbreak of the Second World War was the Nazi-Soviet Pact signed on 24 August 1939. This agreement between Germany and Russia stated that the two countries would attack and divide Poland between them and would not go to war with each other. The agreement with Russia meant that Germany was then free to attack in the west and need not fear a war on two fronts as had happened in 1914. As a result of the treaty Germany would gain half of Poland, which would strengthen it territorially. It also meant that Britain and France, who had signed a treaty to protect Poland, would have to come to its defence and this would lead to a European war. Hitler hoped that because they would not have the support of Russia that Britain and France would not take such action and that he would be free to fight a local war and therefore he invaded Poland on 1 September 1939. Britain and France however did support Poland and declared war on Germany on 3 September, starting a general European war.

The extract explains the role that the Nazi-Soviet Pact and Hitler's subsequent invasion of Poland played in the outbreak of the war, but it does not discuss the importance of the Pact as a factor. How important the Pact was in explaining the outbreak of war is a different task to simply explaining how the Pact led to war.

In order to reach the higher levels you would need to analyse the importance of the Pact in bringing about war.

Producing the right type of paragraph

Read the following paragraph in response to the same question:

> In the context of the years 1848–1939, how far was the outbreak of the Second World War due to long-term German expansionism?

The signing of the Nazi–Soviet Non-aggression Pact was the most important reason why the Second World War broke out in Europe in September 1939. Its short-term significance in starting the war is seen most clearly in that the Pact was signed only on 24 August and just over a week later Britain and France had declared war against Germany. The Pact was crucial in the timing of Hitler's invasion of Poland, which is what led to the outbreak of war, as it meant that Hitler was no longer faced with the possibility of a war on two fronts. He was determined to avoid the same problems that had befallen Imperial Germany in 1914, and therefore once he had secured Russian non-aggression this gave him the confidence to attack Poland. Therefore, although he had been planning the attack on Poland for some time, certainly since the annexation of Czechoslovakia in March 1939, it was only with the certainty that Russia would not join Britain and France that he was willing to go to war, even if he did not expect Britain and France to aid Poland and start a major conflagration.

Compare this paragraph with the one on page 50 in answer to the same question. This response would reach a much higher level than the paragraph on page 50.

Using a coloured pen highlight what information there is in this paragraph that is not in the response on page 50.

What is better about the paragraph on this page than the one on page 50?

_____

_____

The paragraph on this page starts to discuss the relative importance of the Nazi–Soviet Pact in bringing about the Second World War in Europe. This is done through the use of evaluative words.

Make a list of the evaluative words and phrases that are used in the paragraph to argue that the Pact was important.

_____

_____

My progress

Once you have written a paragraph in response to your own question, make a list of the evaluative words that are used to argue that one factor is more important.

Annotate your paragraph to show the sections in which you offer evaluation.

Highlight any areas in which you convey knowledge and explain how they are linked to proving an argument.

5.6 Keeping focus on the set question

One of the main demands of the first Assessment Objective (AO1) is that you remain focused on the question. Once you start to lose focus you will find yourself slipping down the levels. It is therefore really important that you always check that you are answering the question.

Consider the following question.

> How far was the German state the most important factor in the improvement of the rights of women in the years 1899–1989?

A good answer would establish the German state's aims towards women in this period and would consider whether these aims were achieved. Read the following paragraph written in answer to this question.

> The Nazis introduced a considerable number of policies aimed specifically at women. The first of these policies was brought in during June 1933 when women were offered interest-free loans if they married and gave up work. The drive to encourage women to leave work continued with Labour Exchanges encouraged to discriminate in favour of men when they were looking for work rather than giving jobs to women. Policies were also brought in to limit the education opportunities of girls as in January 1934 the number who were allowed to enter higher education was limited and this was further reduced in 1937. Meanwhile, grammar school education for girls was abolished and they were banned from studying Latin which was a requirement for university and this restriction therefore prevented them from applying.

Such a paragraph would not achieve a high mark as it is not focused on the success of German policies towards women. Instead it simply describes some of the policies that the Nazis implemented. If this type of approach continued throughout the response it would place the answer in one of the low mark bands as there is little focus on 'most important'.

Ways an answer can lose focus

There are a number of ways in which an answer can lose focus.

- It can be descriptive of policy or events rather than analytical.
- The material in the paragraph may be relevant to the topic but not the question.

Another way in which an answer can lose focus is to answer a different question. Consider the following question and sample paragraph beneath it:

> To what extent was ideology to blame for the worsening relations between the USA and Russia/Soviet Union in the years 1917–2000?

> The Cold War was caused by ideological differences that can be traced back to the Russian Revolution of 1917. The western powers were fearful of communism spreading to other nations, particularly with the Soviet view of 'world revolution'. However, the Soviet Union felt threatened as it was the only communist country and was surrounded by capitalist states. The Soviet Union and western powers also had different views of the ways in which the economy should be run, with the West supporting capitalism and the Soviet Union wanting it to be under state control. These differing ideologies inevitably led to conflict once the common enemy of Germany had been defeated in 1945.

In this instance the answer focuses on the causes of the Cold War and does not really make an explicit link to the set question. There is some material here that is relevant, but it plainly needs much more development – for example, why should different attitudes to running the economy lead to worsening relations between the USA and the Soviet Union?

Eliminating irrelevance

Perhaps one of the hardest things to do is to ensure that the whole paragraph remains focused on the question and that there are no sentences or sections of a paragraph that are not relevant. Consider the following question and then read the paragraph below in answer to it.

How important was control of the seas in the outcome of British foreign policy in the years 1756–1856?

Napoleon never saw the importance of sea power and suffered as a result. His genius was in land warfare and here rapid movement and concentration of force was the key. He attempted this at Trafalgar but the joint Franco-Spanish fleet was defeated by Nelson. ~~Napoleon could not invade Britain but he had already given up this idea and marched his invasion force from Boulogne to the Danube where he defeated Austria. Britain's coalitions could not withstand Napoleon's forces.~~ However, the supremacy of the navy allowed Britain to control the seas and blockade France, hitting French trade and war supplies. It also meant that Britain could supply and reinforce its forces in the key war in Portugal and Spain, which drained many French resources. ~~This war had begun as a result of Napoleon's desire for even more European expansion. The Spanish resisted and Napoleon was drawn into a long conflict – the 'Spanish ulcer'. This did not deter him from embarking on another war against Austria in 1809.~~

The crossed out sections have no real relevance to the issue being discussed in the paragraph and would be seen as a 'loss of focus'.

Now consider the following question and paragraph and highlight or draw a line through the information that is irrelevant and explain your deletions by annotating the paragraph.

'The ministers served the Crown well, but served themselves better.' How valid is this view of English government in the years 1509–1603?

Cromwell's fall from power in 1540 was the result of many factors. He had served Henry well, had been the architect behind the measures that resulted in the break with Rome and had secured the Royal Supremacy, but this was similar to Cardinal Wolsey who achieved a great deal for Henry. Cromwell had probably achieved more for the King than any other royal servant, bringing about what has been described as a revolution in government and making Henry wealthy through the Dissolution of the Monasteries. Despite many achievements, he had alienated many among the nobility because of his background. His position was further weakened by factional struggles between the religious reformists, which Cromwell represented, and the more Catholic faction under Norfolk and Gardiner, which emerged triumphant following the disastrous Cleves marriage, which Cromwell had been responsible for organising. Howard was able to use his attractive niece, Catherine Howard, to woo Henry and persuade him to believe stories he was told about Cromwell. Cromwell's humble background meant that his entire position at Court relied on the favour of the King, but undoubtedly he was an ambitious individual; this would explain his rapid rise to power.

My progress

Ensure that you check all of your paragraphs to ensure that they are answering the actual question set. You should do this as you write each paragraph. Go back to your question and ask yourself in what ways is this answering the question and are there any parts that are not directly answering it. Delete those parts that are not directly relevant.

5.7 Integrating primary sources and interpretations

Primary sources and interpretations should be integrated into the overall argument being advanced. In this way, the sources and interpretations provide further evidence to support your answer. There should not therefore be a separate section in which the **analysis** of the sources and the interpretations occurs without any attempt to link to the judgement. The key here is to prove that you have not accepted the materials at face value but have evaluated them as to how convincing or how valuable they are in advancing your own answer.

Let's have a look at an example on Anglo-Saxon England where this has been done.

> How significant was the influence of the Great Families in the government of England in the context of the years 978–1066?

Edward the Confessor was the Anglo-Saxon king who died in 1066. There was a powerful noble family, the Godwins, in his kingdom and historians have debated about how far the Godwins undermined his authority and created problems for him. A lot depends on how certain primary evidence is interpreted.

The historian Campbell has a view similar to that of Hill, that there was a revolt in 1051 by the Godwins with the aim of 'changing the king's plans for the succession'. This plan was to make William of Normandy his heir. This would have indicated a considerable amount of influence. However, this view can be challenged. There is no evidence that William of Normandy visited England until after the Godwin family had been exiled and the source for the visit, Florence of Worcester, merely says that William came and was 'entertained honourably'. There is no record of his being made the heir. Campbell and Hill rely on Norman sources such as William of Poitiers

and William of Jumieges who assert, in the words of William of Poitiers, 'Edward loved William as a brother or a son'. However, these sources were written after 1070. By that time William of Normandy had invaded England, killed Harold Godwinson, and was eager to be seen as the rightful heir of the childless Edward. Thus the Norman sources may not give an objective picture and the historians who make too much use of them may be overstating the commitment of Edward to making William his heir and hence the importance of the Godwins in seemingly undermining this.

- In terms of AO1 this is directly focused on the question and discusses a key point about the influence of the great families. The issue **debated** here is whether the Godwins tried to influence the succession.
- In terms of AO2, there is some critical view of the Norman sources, which places their writings in context.
- In terms of AO3 the historians are evaluated by considering what they base their evidence on.

Thus in one paragraph all three assessment objectives are met. Of course, the evaluation could be taken further, but this is an example of how primary and secondary source evaluation can be integrated into the main argument.

This paragraph shows that it is possible to integrate all three objectives into one sustained piece of writing. This is a high-order skill and is an example of a very well-constructed NEA. Do not, however, feel that you need to do this consistently throughout your NEA. It is something useful to aspire towards.

Integrating sources and interpretations

Look at this section from an answer to the following question:

In the context of the years 1857–1947, how far was Indian independence the result of long term economic factors?

The Indian Mutiny in 1857 destroyed a fairly amicable relationship between London and India and led directly to a growing demand for independence. Indeed, the decision to remove control of India from the East India Company is evidence of how much the British wished to suppress the growing tide of resentment felt in India. Historians such as Richard Gott and Lawton report the view of Savarkar in suggesting that the mutiny was so important that it represents the First War of Indian Independence. This however has been countered by Wagner's and Lacey's support of the view that this should be better known as 'The Marginal Mutiny' as its geographical range was so limited. While there is disagreement about the scope of the mutiny there is consensus about the political consequence as seen in Victoria being proclaimed Empress in 1877.

- AO1 – there is some attempt to link to the set question in the opening sentence. However, this is mainly focused on the consequences of a particular action and not the reasons for it.

- AO2 – there is no reference to AO2, which is absolutely fine as it is not expected that all sections of the NEA will use primary sources.

- AO3 – there is little attempt to evaluate the views of the historians. To simply state that they all agree does not make the interpretations convincing or not. The views are identified but that is all. There is no attempt to go beyond this as is required by AO3.

How could this section be improved?

1 How could the material be linked more directly to the reasons for Indian independence?

_____

_____

2 What does the answer need to do to explain and assess the historians' views more?

_____

_____

My progress

Write a paragraph on your own chosen title which integrates sources and shows some evaluation of them. If you can, try to integrate a piece of primary evidence and also a piece of secondary evidence. Check how well you have done by taking account of the following questions:

1 What is the primary evidence?

2 How is it evaluated?

3 What is the secondary evidence?

4 How is it evaluated?

5 What shows you are linking the source to your actual question?

5.8 Evaluation of factors

An evaluation of factors means giving a value to the factors that you have discussed. This means that instead of simply providing a list of reasons as to why, for example, the American Revolution occurred you would weigh up the relative importance of the factors in causing the American Revolution.

Learning how to give a value or explain how important a particular factor is in explaining an event is not an easy skill to master. If you have been accustomed to using spider diagrams in your work you may have slipped into the pattern of simply listing events.

Let's consider how you might approach evaluating the factors for the following topic.

'The coming to power of the Nazi Party in 1933 was due to the growth of militarism in the German states.' How far do you agree with this view of the years 1815–1933?

If you were considering the material dealing with only the short-term factors in your answer then you might think of the factors that are in the table at the bottom of the page.

If you just used the information in the second column of the table you would explain the reasons why Hitler came to power, but the information in the third column gives a value or evaluates the importance of those factors.

You might find it even more helpful to add another column in which you give each factor a mark out of six depending on its importance in increasing Nazi support.

You might then do the same in considering the long-term factors. Remember that you need to ensure that you show understanding across the full date range set in your question.

You must also remember that you need to be able to support your decision. It is no good simply saying it is the most important reason as that is just assertion, you need to explain **why** it is the most important and that is where the information in the third column is vital. Anyone could put numbers from 1 to 6 in a final column. It is your knowledge and understanding of the factors that will allow you to justify your ranking of the factors.

Factor	Explanation of role	Evaluation of importance
1 Rise in unemployment	Growth in Nazi support after Wall Street Crash, not done well before, offered solutions and appeal to those who had lost jobs	Most important because it was only after the growth in unemployment following WSC that support in elections grew
2 Failure of Weimar	Government's inability to agree on policies means they look weak so people turn to other parties	Weimar's inability to deal with unemployment encouraged people to look for an alternative party and they turned to Nazis, therefore quite important
3 Leadership of Hitler	Hitler appeals to many with his oratory, but is also portrayed as a superman who can solve problems, compared with weakness of Weimar	Hitler was able to play on fears of unemployed in his oratory, weakness of Weimar and fear of communism so quite important, but without unemployment and weakness he would not have appealed
4 Reorganisation of Nazi Party	Party is reorganised 1923–24, local leaders are well-trained and able to take advantage of situation	The reorganisation allowed them to take advantage of factors 1 and 2
5 Fear of communism	People did not want similar events to those in Russia so turned to Nazis rather than communists when looking for an alternative	They could have taken advantage of factors 1 and 2 and appealed to unemployed but Hitler's leadership is better and people fear communism after events
6 Propaganda	Able to exploit the situation and portray Hitler as saviour	Used to exploit factors 1, 2, 3 and 5 but without other factors would have been little use

My progress

Now complete a table for your own question which evaluates the importance of the factors or issues you will consider.

My NEA question:

_____

_____

Issue or factor	Explanation	Evaluation	Rank	Justification

5.8 Evaluation of factors

AQA A-level History   57

5.9 Judgement

It is helpful to make interim judgements as you write your essay which should lead you to make an overall judgement based on the critical use of evidence. This is part of good essay technique and should also help you when writing the essay answers in both the examined units. The question you have chosen should lead you to making a judgement which should be firmly placed in a context of about 100 years. You have not asked, for instance, 'Describe the Battle of Hastings' because that does not involve the higher level skill of making a judgement, nor does it place a judgement within a c100-year context. You have not asked 'In the context of the years 978–1066, explain why William the Conqueror managed to seize the throne of England' as that could just be a series of explanations, not a judgement. You might have asked 'In the context of the years 978–1066, assess the reasons why William of Normandy managed to seize the throne of England' as 'assess' involves a judgement – which reason or reasons were the most important? You need to reach a judgement even if it is qualified. Here are some examples.

During the Battle of Hastings on 14 October 1066 the Saxon forces formed a powerful shield wall on higher ground. The Normans attacked but could not break the line, but seeing the Normans give way, the Saxons broke ranks and pursued them, leaving themselves vulnerable to counterattack.

Thus, though the evidence shows that Harold's men were likely to have been exhausted by their previous fighting and their long march and this may have been a factor, it does not fully explain the outcome. The Saxon forces maintained their battle line effectively against Norman attacks and were confident enough to try to make the victory decisive by pursuing the Normans not once, but twice. This does not suggest over-weary troops but, if anything, an excess of enthusiasm and vigour which was misapplied. It was William's ability to take advantage of this that was more important.

This one factor cannot be a total explanation, but this 'clinching' judgement would certainly help towards a strong overall conclusion.

Now compare this answer with the sample below on the French Revolution.

> How far were any gains made in the French Revolution reversed in the context of the years 1789–1871?

Napoleon Bonaparte was a successful general who took over France in 1799 ending the rule of the Directory which had governed from 1795. That government had been purged of its enemies on several occasions. Napoleon introduced plebiscites (referenda) to ask the electorate its opinion of issues, but the results were manipulated.

In terms of politics, Napoleon could be seen as destroying democracy and meaningful universal male suffrage. All men over 21 could vote but they had to vote for candidates approved by the state. It could be said though that Napoleon did at least keep elements of the Constitution and did not make himself dictator. Sutherland uses the evidence of the rigged plebiscites and sees him introducing dictatorship, but Jordan questions whether it was in fact Napoleon who destroyed democracy because of the coup of Fructidor under the Directory, which together with other purges undermined meaningful democracy. However, Napoleon himself said 'the constitution means nothing to me', though this might not be typical of his views as he tried to introduce a more liberal constitution, later.

There is some good material here, but it really needs a judgement. What does this really show? Where is the balance? What is the final conclusion going to be? What does the writer think after looking at this evidence?

Interim judgements

A

Look again at the paragraph on Napoleon on page 58. Which of these interim judgements do you think might be made on the basis of the evidence in the paragraph?

1 Thus, Napoleon definitely destroyed the gains of the Revolution in terms of democracy and constitutional government.

Is this valid?

_____

_____

_____

2 Napoleon did not destroy the gains of the Revolution because he consulted the people in plebiscites and had universal male suffrage.

Is this valid?

_____

_____

_____

3 Napoleon did not completely destroy the gains of the Revolution in the sense that there was still a constitution and the gains had already been undermined by the previous revolutionary regime. However, he undermined any real hopes for a democratic and constitutional rule by restricting the candidates to be voted for and by rigging plebiscites so though he kept a pretence of continuity he actually undermined the gains made.

Is this valid?

_____

_____

_____

My progress

Take a section of your essay and write a clear interim judgement. It should present a clear view of the issue in the question.

_____

5.10 Example coursework paragraphs

Here are some examples of sections from answers. Underneath each one there is a commentary that you can use to check your initial thoughts.

'William the Conqueror was successful in seizing the throne of England because of the weaknesses of the English state.' How valid is this view of the years 978–1066?

Huscroft argues that William succeeded because of the lack of English troops and William's leadership on the battlefield. Golding doesn't say what he thinks is the key reason for the outcome but he thinks that William's army was born of a practical necessity and supports Huscroft's view that William and his army were the most important reasons. However, these views don't take into account Harold's actions. Walker on the other hand thinks that Harold was beaten 'by a better man'; and Hill quotes Stenton, saying 'he lost the battle because his men were unequal to the stress'. Hill is more convincing because he looks at the situation before the battle. William of Jumièges says that the English lost because 'they lost confidence' and William of Poitiers doesn't agree. Therefore it is clear that Harold was the most important factor.

There are a number of historians quoted here but they are not well analysed in terms of the explanations they offer. Just because Golding agrees with Huscroft this does not make their view correct and in any case the basis of it is not explained. There is virtually no evaluation except for the statement that the views don't take into account Harold's actions, but this is not explained. This comes close to just describing what different people have said which really is a typical Level 2 response. The opportunities to assess the primary evidence are not taken and the explanations lack clarity. The answer seems very keen to bring in a lot of sources but needs to sort out the arguments and try to assess the evidence. A lot of work seems to be behind this, but it needs to step back and look more carefully at the evidence.

In the context of the years 1487–1601, how far were Tudor risings motivated by religious discontent?

Dickens has dismissed the pilgrims' religious motive and accused them of being incapable of staging Wars of Religion. What seems to contradict this is that nine out of 24 of the Pontefract Articles deal with religion. However, these articles might have been used to disguise personal and political issues. They were produced not by the common people but by educated elites who had more than just religious grievances. Haigh has also argued that 'the economic concerns of the people and the legal and political concerns of the leaders could have been cloaked by the religious language of the Articles. The economic stresses of the North might support this view. The harvest of 1535 had been bad and the genuine religious concerns of the Articles can be questioned by consideration that the banning of the sales of indulgences was not mentioned. However, the religious symbolism of the pilgrimage, the obvious idealism of Aske shown when he was being questioned after his arrest and the appearance of religious concerns in the majority of the Pontefract Articles mean that it cannot be convincing to take such a strong line as Dickens does about the nature of the pilgrimage.

This has a critical approach to both primary and secondary evidence and is firmly focused on the issue in the question, coming to an interim conclusion at the end.

My progress

Here is a checklist to help evaluate the quality of your paragraphs.

- Does the paragraph use primary source material or interpretations? Not every paragraph needs to.
- Is the view of the sources or interpretations made clear if they are included?
- Are there any judgements made about the evidence?
- Is the judgement based on any evidence or simply asserted?
- Is the paragraph relevant to the title?
- Is there an interim judgement based on the discussion?

Write a paragraph from your essay that deals with primary sources or interpretations and then complete the checklist.

Does the paragraph use source material? If so where?

Are there primary and secondary sources? What are they?

Is the view of the sources made clear? Give one example.

Are there any judgements made about the evidence? Give one example.

Is the judgement based on any evidence or simply asserted? Give one example.

Is the paragraph relevant to the title? How can you be sure?

Is there an interim judgement based on the discussion? What shows that?

5.11 Writing a conclusion

The conclusion should be based on the interim judgements made throughout the essay if it is going to be convincing. If all the evidence points to, for example, Charles I being the cause of the English Civil War, then that should be the basis of the conclusion. It is no good suddenly saying in the conclusion that all this didn't matter as Charles was the victim of the ambition of MPs in Parliament. That should have been considered in the essay, not the conclusion. There is an old-fashioned idea that you need to produce something different and exciting in the conclusion to avoid your essay being 'boring'. This is not true. A conclusion that suddenly reverses all the arguments made in the bulk of the essay simply seems jarring to the reader and suggests that you have been ignoring key counter arguments. If you have proposed a clear line of argument at the start, the conclusion should confirm that, even if there may be modifications and qualifications.

This is an essay, not something that is going to be set in stone or used for a definite statement on the issue. It should reflect your search for the truth based on the evidence that you have accessed. If you had more time, more space and more sources then it is possible that your conclusions might need to be revised. If you rewrote it at university then you might change your view. Historians are not afraid, if they have real integrity, of modifying their views or even changing their minds as a result of further evidence. All history, perhaps all knowledge, represents interim judgements not fixed conclusions. So please don't shy away from judgements, provided they are supported by the evidence and are the result of careful thought and analysis. With the type of questions you are tackling, there is often no 'right' or 'wrong' answer. So do offer a concluding judgement, even if it is hedged about.

This conclusion to the question 'How important was religion in causing Tudor Rebellion in the years 1487–1601?' is a good example of a clear but balanced view.

Considering all the reasons for unrest it would be right to argue that a combination of factors brought about rebellion. Though the main causes were economic and social it was religion that provided the essential element that bound them together. Without religion the other reasons would not have been strong enough to lead the rebels to the very dangerous path of challenging the king's authority. However, rebellion was not motivated by religious change in general, as this had been going on throughout the period. It was above all a protest about the specific religious policy of the dissolution of the monasteries and later of change on a local level, because it was that part of the reformation that was most closely linked to social and economic concerns. The political causes were important, but these could not have been the most important as the majority of those caught up in rebellion were commoners and matters of politics mainly concerned the nobles and the educated classes.

Writing conclusions

Look again at the conclusion on page 62. Identify the answer to the question it gives.

_____

_____

Now look at this example of part of the conclusion to the question 'How important was US public opinion in the direction of US foreign policy in the twentieth century?'

> Some historians have emphasised public opinion as the key factor in US foreign policy. This was especially true in Vietnam when the accessibility of images from the war in people's homes was important and led to some opposition which made it necessary for the politicians to bring the war to an end. This was also made important by military problems, as it had not proved possible to decisively defeat the Vietcong because of the way they fought and their deep commitment. In addition, US public opinion was carefully manipulated in the Second World War through government propaganda agencies. Later, the idea of embedding the media within troop units became popular as it gave an insight into the type of dangers and fighting that US soldiers were experiencing.

Can you identify the answer to the question?

_____

_____

Had the question been 'Explain the reasons …' then this would have been a valid conclusion but it is difficult to pick out the answer from the conclusion. This is rather a jumble of disconnected points, perhaps treating the conclusion as more of a summary than an argued piece.

My progress

Write a possible conclusion to your question – it doesn't matter if you haven't finished the research. Just try to form an opinion on what you've done so far.

Which of the two examples in this section is it most like?

_____

_____

Why?

_____

_____

Bibliography and footnotes

In carrying out your research for the NEA you will have seen that many of the books and articles that you have used contain footnotes at the bottom of the page, or endnotes at the end of each chapter in which authors acknowledge other works from which they obtained their information and do not try to claim that it is their own research.

Similarly, at the end of the book there will be a bibliography. This is somewhat different from footnotes or endnotes. A bibliography is a list of all the books that authors have referred to during their research, even if they have not quoted from them or taken ideas and information from them.

Both of these should appear in your NEA. There are a number of reasons for this:

- You need to show where you obtained the knowledge, sources and Interpretations that you are using.
- You cannot claim that ideas and knowledge are your own when they have been taken from other people's work. That is plagiarism.
- It is an academic convention and this is an academic piece of work.
- It is good practice for the future as higher education institutions will expect it.

Bibliography

Although the bibliography appears at the end of your essay it might be a good idea to start with it because it is a record of all the works you have read in order to write your essay. This means that you need to keep a record of your reading as you go along as you will never remember all that you have read when you have finished the work! Even if you could, it would be very time consuming to have to go back to find out all the titles, authors and other details that are needed to put together a bibliography.

What should the bibliography contain and how should it be set out?

The bibliography should be a record of all the works you have referred to when doing your research, including primary sources, secondary sources, articles and collections of essays and any visual or audio materials.

These works are not simply lumped together in a list, but are normally organised into sections with headings:

- Primary Sources
- Secondary Sources
- Articles and Collections of Essays
- Other Materials.

Within each section the work is ordered alphabetically according to the surname of the author, and will contain the author's name, the title of the book, the publisher and the date of publication:

Pope, R., *War and Society in Britain*, Longman, London, 1991

In terms of books with more than one author then the following should be used:

Dicken, M. and Fellows, N., *Britain 1603–1760*, Hodder, London, 2015

When there is an editor:

Boyce, D. and O'Day, A. (eds.) *Parnell in Perspective*, Routledge, London, 1991

With articles from journals:

Goodlad, G., Feb 2013, 'Margaret Thatcher and the Soviet Union', *Twentieth Century History Review*, vol 8., no 3, pages 26–29

With other materials, such as web pages, the format is again different. The most basic entry for a website consists of the author name(s), page title, website title, sponsoring institution/publisher, date published, medium and date accessed.

With websites it is crucial that you keep a note of the date accessed as the site may change over time. Do remember that your secondary sources will need to be published in print – being published on a website is not enough.

If you use a writing tool such as OneNote or Evernote to collect your material from websites then it will copy down the URL address and date accessed automatically for you.

You may discover that different institutions require different formats. AQA does not stipulate a particular style as long as you are consistent in using the same version throughout your NEA.

Footnotes

All the books and articles, etc., that appear in the footnotes should appear in the bibliography, but the format will be different.

Footnotes acknowledge where you have used information from another source and show that you are not claiming it to be your own. With computers it is very easy to insert the number in the text and the reference at the bottom of the page (or at the end of the work if you are using endnotes). The computer will also ensure that the footnotes are in numerical order. Once again there is a wide range of different styles, but it would make sense if they were in a similar format to the bibliography.

The main differences between footnotes and the bibliography are that the footnote will start with the first name of the author(s) and it includes the page or pages from which you have drawn your information:

Rex Pope, *War and Society in Britain*, (Longman, London, 1991) pages 48–49.

Footnotes can also be used to add further information which, if included in the main body of the NEA, would spoil the flow. However, if the information is important to your argument then it should be in the main body of the essay!

If you use the same book or article consecutively then you may simply put:

ibid page 50

Similarly, if the same book is used later in your essay you do not need to write out the full details but can simply put the name of the author and the page used.

Your Centre may have a policy on the system they want you to use and it would be worth checking to see before following the guidance given here. AQA has no set requirement of the system that is used, but consistency is the key.

Research skills and plagiarism

Plagiarism is pretending that someone else's work is your own. It is unlikely that students will download a ready-made essay from a website and say they wrote it, but sites that offer essays for a fee should be avoided. It is also unlikely that students will get someone else to write their coursework, as this is dishonest and also teachers would see that the work was clearly not that of someone they had taught and whose work they knew. However, a great deal of material is available on websites and can be copied and pasted easily. Textbooks, articles and specialist studies can be photocopied or photographed. Many students like to build up a body of material like this, but it is very important when researching that there is a distinction between work read, consulted, used and made part of their own work as opposed to material that is just inserted without any acknowledgement. That sort of plagiarism is not as obvious as the use of someone else's whole work but it is just as important to avoid it.

The use of books and articles

When research is undertaken it is vital for notes to be made that get to the heart of ideas, arguments and supporting factual information. If a particular argument is used then it is often helpful to quote briefly but long extracts should be avoided and essays should not consist of a series of quotations. When a direct quote is made then this should be footnoted with the page reference in the book. If an idea is taken from a history book then it should also be acknowledged. It would obviously not be appropriate to acknowledge where you obtained every fact. If you are starting without previous knowledge, let's say of the Battle of Hastings, and you read a history book or article that tells you it was on 14 October 1066, then you would not acknowledge where you got this information as it is common knowledge. However, if you decide to take a particular argument about the battle's outcome from a book or article then this should be acknowledged. You are using someone else's research and ideas and they will be happy that their work is being read and used – but it is common academic courtesy to acknowledge that it is their idea that you are using and not your own. The marks at the higher levels come from expressing a clear and consistent answer – it is very difficult to do this if you are simply attempting to put someone else's views in your own words.

The use of primary evidence

To introduce an opinion or explanation from a primary source is not quite the same, but it is necessary to reference the evidence by a footnote to show where the argument came from and to make clear that the interpretation is not yours but is taken from a source.

The use of internet material

This material can often be copied very easily. It is extremely important that sections of work are not unacknowledged lifting from online encyclopaedias or articles. As with books it is strongly recommended that notes are taken from the material and that arguments and ideas are acknowledged. If there is a quotation then the web address and the date of accessing the site should be included.

The use of secondary evidence

Many books outline the historiography of the topic they are dealing with. This is often very helpful in coursework, but students should not give the impression that they have read and used the sources mentioned and should acknowledge that they are using an account of different views by an author, not that they have consulted the historians mentioned when they have not.

For example, in preparing an answer to the question

> In the context of the years 1775 to 1861, how far was the American Civil War caused by weaknesses in the US Constitution?

a student has found this overview of the historiography:

Source A: Alan Farmer, *Access to History: America, Civil War and Westward Expansion* (Hodder Education, 2015, pages 108–9)

In the 1920s, 'progressive' historians claimed that clashes between interest groups underpinned events in history, and suggested that the war was a contest between plantation agriculture and industrialising capitalism. According to progressives, economic issues (such as the tariff) were what really divided the power-brokers – northern manufacturers and southern planters. The confederacy could thus be seen as fighting for the preservation of a stable, agrarian civilisation in the face of the grasping ambitions of northern businessmen … In the 1940s, revisionist historians denied that sectional conflicts, whether over slavery, state rights or industry versus agriculture were genuinely divisive e.g. the differences between North and South, wrote revisionist historian Avery Craven, were 'no greater than those existing at different times between East and West'. In the revisionist view, far more united than divided the two sections: sectional quarrels could and should have been accommodated peacefully. Far from being irrepressible, the war was brought on by extremists on both sides … Historians have now come full circle. The progressive and revisionist schools are currently dormant. Lincoln's view that slavery was 'somehow' the cause of the war is generally accepted. While the Confederacy might claim its justification to be the protector of state rights, in truth, it was one state right – the right to preserve slavery – that impelled the Confederate states' separation. Slavery defined the South, permeating every aspect.

The passage above is a highly useful survey of different ideas. It gives a starting point for the student to find different interpretations and to test them. However, its style is not necessarily the style of an A-level student. An essay that is plagiarised might begin like this:

> There are many different reasons for the Civil War. 'Progressive' historians have claimed that clashes between different interest groups caused the war. They have claimed that the war was a contest between plantation owners and industrialising capitalism and war was about issues such as the tariff. However, revisionist historians like Avery Craven had argued that differences were 'no greater than those existing at different times between east and west' and the war was brought on by extremists. These views are now dormant. It is generally accepted that Lincoln's view was right and slavery was 'somehow' the cause as slavery permeated every aspect of the South.

The false impression is given that the writer has read Craven, and the analysis of the historiography, which is Alan Farmer's, is being passed off as the student's own. There are even direct quotations that are not acknowledged. It is fine to get a general idea when you start off the different views, but this is just taking a short cut, which is unethical.

Self-assessment

As this coursework is an independent essay, the amount of help your teacher can give is limited by the rules set down by the body that regulates all A-level examinations. This means that they cannot offer detailed comments and cannot make specific suggestions. Your work is going to be marked against set guidelines, so it is important that you try to apply the mark scheme yourself before you hand in the work in its final form for marking.

If you get used to making use of the mark scheme as you're writing, then this should help you to be sure that you are on the right lines. When you have got your NEA pretty well ready to hand in, you can do a final check.

Looking at your essay, you have to ask yourself whether it meets the requirements. You can do this by filling out the tables below and completing the questions on this double page. Don't wait until the end to fill this in. Once you start writing, refer to it. It would be hard work if you wrote your essay and were ready to hand it in and then went through this list only to find there were no primary sources!

Assessment objectives

AO1 Key questions to ask	Yes/mostly/partly/no	What do I need to do to meet it?
Have I related everything in my essay to the question?		
Have I assessed different explanations or have I just made a one-way argument?		
Have I included a lot of description rather than explaining and assessing?		
Have I included interim judgements?		
Have I made an overall judgement?		
Have I used detailed and specific knowledge?		

AO2 Primary sources	Yes/mostly/partly/no	What do I need to do to meet it?
Have I included at least three primary sources?		
Have I ensured that there are at least two different types of primary source?		
Have I proved that I understand the content of them and used them to support a view?		
Have I evaluated three in depth and come to a judgement about the value of each source?		
Have I considered all aspects of the provenance as appropriate, e.g. author, date, type of source, intended audience?		

AO3 Secondary sources	Yes/mostly/partly/no	What do I need to do to meet it?
Have I included at least two differing interpretations?		
Have I referenced them in footnotes and included them in the bibliography?		
Have I used a reasonable range?		
Have I proved that I understand the content and used this to support a view?		
Have I evaluated each source in terms of time/context written and also limitations facing each historian?		

Use of sources

I have used _____ primary sources in my essay

of _____ different types.

I have used _____ named historians in my essay

of _____ differing views.

Evaluation of evidence

Evaluation means putting a value on the evidence. Please circle how you have evaluated evidence in your essay.

I have evaluated the sources by:

- using my own knowledge
- referring to the provenance of primary sources
- corroborating evidence
- considering what evidence historians have used
- considering the time/context and also limitations of secondary sources.

One way you can check that you are evaluating is to highlight evaluative words in your essay. Check how many of the evaluative words and phrases in the pink box appear in your work when you have referred to primary or secondary sources.

This evidence:
- is/is not valid
- is/is not reliable
- is/is not typical
- is/is not useful
- is/is not complete
- is too reliant on a certain type of evidence
- neglects to take into account …
- overestimates …
- puts too much emphasis on …
- however, (Taylor argues …, however, this …)
- is too influenced
- is/is not supported by
- is/is not corroborated by

Research logs

There is absolutely no requirement from AQA to keep a research log, but it may help you to keep a record of your ideas and your sources. You do need to reference everything you've used, and often you have some good ideas but they get forgotten, so keeping a record helps. It also helps your teacher to see what progress you've been making and to confirm that your final essay is your own work. Below is a suggested format for the different stages of your coursework. The log has been filled in to give you an idea of what to do. As you work on your coursework you can fill out the blank version on pages 72–79.

Getting started – deciding on a topic and making sure your title works

Initial idea for topic based essay	Why I chose it	Initial search for resources
July What caused the US Civil War? Was the South to blame? Was it just slavery? Was Lincoln wrong? Was America destined to fracture from the start? Or Can slavery in the Southern states before 1861 be justified?	I found this interesting in my GCSE course but want to know about this in more depth. We did look at some theories but only for a few lessons. There is a lot of material available and different views to look at. Decided against the question on slavery after discussion with teacher as too much like an ethical question.	Did an internet search on the US Civil War and started to look at A-level texts. Found an Access to History book with a good section on causes. Found websites on the debate.

Refining the question and the sources

Draft title for submission to AQA	Explanation showing different interpretations	Are there primary sources?	Any advice from tutor/ AQA
September In context of the years 1775–1861, why did civil war break out in the USA in 1861? October How far was slavery the main cause of the US Civil War?	Revisionists question importance of deep divisions about slavery and the progressive school think economic factors more important. Changed because the role of slavery gives me a clear starting point.	I found sources on line, for example, Southern states own explanation for secession and Lincoln's speeches in 1861.	In a discussion, teacher suggested that 'why' might lead to a list and that I should make sure that my title leads clearly to a discussion. AQA approved topic but changed the question to 'Assess the view that slavery was the main cause of the US Civil War in the context of 1776–1861.'

Initial interpretations research

Date	Resource	Key ideas	Evaluation
October	Alan Farmer, America: Civil War and Westward Expansion 1803–90 Hodder, 2015	Outlines different theories like Progressives in 1920s arguing for economic issues; Revisionists arguing for just extremists. Book's own view is that slavery was key issue not states' rights because of economic importance.	Need to find more information to justify economic importance of slavery to South to see if view is supported. Question the view – see if slavery really was being threatened or was it just an excuse?

Record of sources used (sample extract from research log)

Date	Tutorial/Seminar	Issues discussed	How this affected my research/writing
October	Seminar on source evaluation.	How primary sources should be evaluated.	I went back to my sources on southern reasons for leaving the union to make sure that I had used them critically.

Sample resource record

Centre Number:

Candidate Name:

Resources used Sources and three interpretations needed	Page/web reference	Student comments	Student date(s) when accessed	Teacher initials and date resource record checked
Alan Farmer America: Civil War and westward Expansion 1803–90 Hodder, 2015*	Pages 23–48	Outlines different theories – progressives in 1920s arguing for economic issues; Revisionists arguing for just extremists. Book's own view is that slavery was key issue not states' rights because of economic importance. Provides a contrasting view to that found in Smith so appropriate as a chosen work.	20 October	
Richard Nicholson The American Civil War Penguin, 1992	Pages 10–29	This study adopts a traditionalist view and looks to states' rights as the most important cause. It is quite broad in its focus and generally emphasises views found in other works from earlier in the 20th century. I decided not to use it as one of my chosen works as it is quite brief and does not consider any new research. I may use it to back up the views of other historians.		

Getting started - deciding on a topic and making sure your title works

Initial idea for essay	Why I chose it	Initial search for resources	Any advice from tutor/ AQA

Initial idea for essay	Why I chose it	Initial search for resources	Any advice from tutor/ AQA

Refining the title and interpretations

Draft title	Explanation showing different interpretations	Supplementary reading	Any advice from tutor

Draft title	Explanation showing different interpretations	Supplementary reading	Any advice from tutor

Initial interpretations research

Date	Resource	Key ideas	Evaluation

Date	Resource	Key ideas	Evaluation

Sample resource record

Centre Number:

Candidate Name:

Resources used The three chosen sources and two interpretations needed	Page/web reference	Student comments	Student date(s) when accessed	Teacher initials and date resource record checked

Resources used The three chosen sources and two interpretations needed	Page/web reference	Student comments	Student date(s) when accessed	Teacher initials and date resource record checked

Research logs

Glossary

Analysis An analysis of the causes or consequences of an event means explaining what brought it or followed from it, not describing the events that led to it or came afterwards.

Argument The thrust of the essay. If the question asks whether Germany was responsible for the First World War an argument will clearly explain whether it was or was not or how far it was responsible and not simply explain the causes of what Germany did.

Assertions Statements made that are not supported by evidence. 'This interpretation is obviously true' is an assertion. 'This interpretation is true because it is supported by ...' is supported analysis and judgement.

Assess This is a command word that requires making a judgement. 'Assess the reasons' means not give the reasons but make a judgement about their importance relative to each other.

Assumptions These are stock views not based on specific knowledge and evidence. For example, 'This source was written by a historian who did not see the event therefore it is unreliable' is based on an assumption that being at an event makes you a reliable witness.

Bibliography A list of all sources used in the essay at the end giving author, title and date. If websites are used the web address and the date accessed should be given.

Conclusion Summing up your view about the question.

Corroborated This is where views and evidence are made more convincing by comparing them with other views and evidence. This is distinct from merely noting that works agree, which is just comparison, but if the view in one work is supported by actual evidence in another source then this is real corroboration.

Debate There are established debates or disagreements about historical issues, for example the lengthy series of arguments for and against the thesis that there was a Tudor Revolution in Government. However, 'debate' can mean a possible discussion about the relative importance of different causes or consequences and the existence of different views about key features of a period not a formal or extended or indeed impassioned historical discussion.

Evaluate This involves weighing and giving a value to historical interpretations or factors. It is distinct from explaining the views and evidence and should be quite clear in these essays by using critical words.

Footnotes Information provided at the bottom of the page about sources used in the text of the essay. Footnotes need to show author, title and date of any sources but should not include information that is part of the argument. This should be in the essay itself.

Interpretations The way that historians explain the past based on their reading of the evidence.

Judgement There should be assessment of evidence and views in order to reach a clear personal view about the topic – judgement is essential even if is tentative. This is an essay and provided your judgement is based on knowledge and evidence you will not be penalised for getting the 'wrong answer'.

Moderators These are examiners who check that school or college marking is in line with national standards and that it is based on a clear understanding of the requirements of the mark scheme.

Narrative Historical accounts of what happened in the past. This is not needed in topic-based essays.

Plagiarism This is cheating by passing off the work of others as your own, for example by downloading essays from the internet and using parts of them without acknowledging where you got them from.

HODDER EDUCATION

t: 01235 827827
e: education@bookpoint.co.uk
w: hoddereducation.co.uk

ISBN 978-1-5104-2352-7